The Prairie in Seed

T0054130

A BUR OAK GUIDE

Holly Carver, series editor

The Prairie in Seed

*Identifying Seed-Bearing Prairie Plants
in the Upper Midwest*

DAVE WILLIAMS

UNIVERSITY OF IOWA PRESS, IOWA CITY

Copyright © 2016 by the University of Iowa Press
www.uiowapress.org
Printed in the United States of America

Design by April Leidig

No part of this book may be reproduced or used in any form or by
any means without permission in writing from the publisher. All
reasonable steps have been taken to contact copyright holders of
material used in this book. The publisher would be pleased to make
suitable arrangements with any whom it has not been possible to
reach.

The University of Iowa Press is a member of Green Press Initiative
and is committed to preserving natural resources.

Printed on acid-free paper

Library of Congress Cataloging-in-Publication Data
Williams, Dave (David Wayne), 1961– author.
The prairie in seed : identifying seed-bearing prairie plants
in the upper Midwest / Dave Williams.
pages   cm. — (Bur Oak guides)
Includes bibliographical references and index.
ISBN 978-1-60938-409-8 (pbk), ISBN 978-1-60938-410-4 (ebk)
1. Prairie plants — Middle West — Identification.
2. Prairie plants — Seeds — Middle West — Identification.
I. Title. II. Title: Identifying seed-bearing prairie plants in the
upper Midwest. III. Series: Bur Oak guide.
QK128.W54   2016
639.9'90977 — dc23   2015028384

Living Roadway Trust Fund of Iowa

This guide was funded by the Iowa Department of
Transportation, Iowa Living Roadway Trust Fund.

Drawings of leaf divisions, shapes, and margins were adapted
from *Plant Identification Terminology: An Illustrated Glossary*
by James G. Harris and Melinda Woolf Harris (Payson, UT:
Spring Lake Publishing, 2004).

To my wife, Maureen,

for her invaluable editorial advice and patience.
I could not have done this book without you.
All my love,
Dave

Contents

PART ONE. Solitary Seed Heads

PART TWO. Seeds in Follicles

Preface and Acknowledgments

· ·

In recent years, the tallgrass prairie has been proven to offer solutions to many environmental challenges associated with our water, soils, and wildlife ecosystem. While cities like Des Moines, Iowa, for example, struggle to control nitrate levels in their drinking water with expensive filtration systems, Iowa State University researchers have found that planting prairie on 10 percent of a field can effectively remove excess phosphorus and nitrogen from the remaining 90 percent (Zhou et al. 2014). We also know that deep prairie roots and dense, aboveground growth work together to filter and hold midwestern soils, effectively keeping them from eroding into our streams and rivers and offering the potential to slow or even stop the expansion of the dead zone in the Gulf of Mexico. More recently, specific native prairie plants such as the common milkweed have been identified as key to recovery for the monarch butterfly, perhaps even keeping it from becoming an endangered species (Pleasants and Oberhauser 2012).

Americans' century-old love affair with European turf grass is slowly giving way to discovery of the benefits and beauty of our original native prairie. Many states enjoy broad public support for revegetating road rights-of-way with prairie wildflowers and grasses in lieu of mowing, which reduces maintenance costs while providing a colorful blooming landscape from early spring through fall. It is common to see prairie plants used in landscaping at city parks throughout the Midwest, on golf courses and along trails, around businesses and industrial parks, and more recently in residential yards as homeowners tire of chemicals, turf maintenance, and a bland green landscape.

As interest in prairie wildflowers and grasses has grown, so has demand for better resources to identify the hundreds of species of wildflowers and grasses that make up the native prairie from the time they emerge as seedlings until they set seeds. In *The Tallgrass Prairie Center Guide to Seed and Seedling Identification in the Upper Midwest* (2010), I documented an initial group of native prairie plant seedlings through photographs, descriptions, and drawings to help prairie advocates identify seedlings in the spring. There are a multitude of excellent books that help identify prairie plants once they are in flower, based on flower color and shape. Once they are out of bloom, however, it can be difficult to spot and identify prairie plants. Without the flower color and shape to guide us, distinguishing between a simple prairie sunflower and an ox-eye sunflower can be almost impossible.

The Prairie in Seed is designed to assist the prairie advocate in identifying wild-flowers once they are out of bloom and, in particular, to support those who harvest prairie seeds. This guide offers dormant plant identification, seed descriptions, and guidance for effective seed harvesting and cleaning for seventy-three of the most common wildflowers found in the tallgrass prairie. I have used *The Vascular Plants of Iowa: An Annotated Checklist and Natural History* by Lawrence J. Eilers and Dean M. Roosa (1994), *An Illustrated Guide to Iowa Prairie Plants* by Paul Christiansen and Mark Müller (1999), and the USDA Natural Resources Conservation Service PLANTS Database for binomial nomenclature.

I would like to thank the University of Northern Iowa Tallgrass Prairie Center (TPC) for giving me the time and equipment to pursue this project. I am sincerely thankful to my colleague Gregory Houseal at the TPC for his botanical expertise and manuscript editing. Thanks to Holly Carver and Karen Copp at the University of Iowa Press for editing and design work on the manuscript. This guide was funded by the Iowa Department of Transportation, Iowa Living Roadway Trust Fund.

Remember to get permission if you are harvesting seeds on private or public property, and do not harvest in an area designated as a preserve. Good harvesting ethics is to take only half and leave half on the site. Good luck!

Of Photographs and Fieldwork

. . . .

I took all the photographs in this book with an 8-megapixel digital Canon Rebel XT camera with a fixed 50 mm lens for full plant shots and a 100 mm macro lens for close-up shots. Photographs were taken at the Cedar Hills Sand Prairie Preserve in Black Hawk County, Iowa; at Clay Prairie Preserve in Butler County, Iowa; and at a forty-two-year-old prairie reconstruction on the campus of the University of Northern Iowa in Cedar Falls. I used a golf umbrella attached to a large tripod to regulate sunlight.

This book was two years in the making. During that time, I visited the prairies and plants showcased in this book multiple times, hoping for favorable light and low winds. Each and every time I was in the field, I was rewarded. In addition to witnessing amazing sunrises and sunsets, I had an encounter with a bobcat in a county park, watched a bumblebee burst from a bottle gentian while I was focusing my camera lens, and had a humbling encounter with dozens of monarchs. Probably most memorable was the morning I found myself dodging bullets from a nearby shooting range while seeking plants to flag in eastern Iowa.

With seventy-three distinct species to track, this was a complicated project. In September, I set out to photograph showy goldenrod in bloom. I was pleasantly surprised to find more than twenty monarch butterflies foraging on this species. My first thought was, "What a great opportunity to photograph my target species with a monarch on the flower." I carefully approached a plant with a monarch feeding. As I came close, the butterfly spooked and flew around me, landing on another showy goldenrod just out of the photograph zone. This happened over and over. They were hungry, and I was in their space. I settled for a long photo shot, grateful for the opportunity to share their space.

One week in May, I visited Cedar Hills Sand Prairie, intending to flag a prairie violet so I could find it again when it was in flower and in seed. After nearly three frustrating hours of searching, I called Daryl Smith, the founding director of the Tallgrass Prairie Center, and asked him if he knew where those violets were located. "Sure, Dave," he said. "Go about fifty yards southeast from the gate and look down. They will be right there." I followed Daryl's directions, and right at my feet was a prairie violet. Amazing.

I realized in January that I had overlooked collecting seeds from wild petunia when they were ripe back in early October. Facing the possibility of not including this species in the book, I went back out onto the cold prairie looking for a six-inch-high petunia. Thanks to my detailed field notes, I was able to find a petunia, and to my surprise it appeared that all of the capsules were intact and still connected to the stalk. I harvested some of the capsules, put them into an open paper bag, and went back to my office, placing the bag on my desk. About an hour later, I heard a large pop, then another, then another. As the capsules from the wild petunia warmed up, the shells were exploding — sending seeds ricocheting off the inside of the bag! I looked at the inside of each capsule half and found a small lever with a spring that, when pushed with my finger, sprang into the air. It appears that when the capsule warms up, the spring lever breaks it in half and ejects the seeds. The wild petunia holds its seeds on the stalk throughout the winter until warm spring days cause capsules to eject their seeds onto the ground to start the process of developing new plants.

Please enjoy this book. I hope that you have as much fun identifying prairie plants and collecting their seeds.

How to Use This Guide

Each species in this guide includes photographs and descriptions of the plants in bloom and in seed to assist in finding them when you are ready to harvest. Each species description explains where the seeds are located on the plant, when seed ripening begins, and how many seeds are produced, along with approximate measurements of the actual seed. The In Seed photos show seed capsules or pods, not seeds; some photos may also include a capsule or husk. For some species, small colored triangles in the photos correspond to statements in the text marked with triangles. Finally, this guide provides assistance on how and when to hand-harvest seeds for each species and some simple tips on seed cleaning.

The easiest way to locate a plant of a given species is to visit the site when the plant is in flower and document its location, usually with a flag, so you can find it later when it is in seed. See table 1 to find a list of flowering times for the seventy-three wildflower species in this book. The species are grouped in this table by flowering times to ripening times. These dates are the result of observed average flowering times for two consecutive growing seasons in northeast Iowa. Keep in mind that these dates are approximate and can vary by a few weeks based on weather conditions (cold weather prolongs flowering; hot weather hastens flowering) and latitude (flowering occurs sooner in the season in the northern tallgrass prairie region and later in the season to the south).

You may also use this book to identify an unknown plant and its seeds based on stalk, seed head, and seeds. Locate the dried flower/seed head of your unknown plant; then follow it down the stem to where it connects to the main stalk. Plants can be distinguished by how the seed heads connect to the main stalk. Keep in mind that seed heads come in many different shapes: a single or solitary head, follicles (in milkweeds), leaf axils, racemes, spikes, umbels, or panicles with or without pappus bristles. The glossary has a detailed description of each type of seed head. Choose a stalk with an intact seed head of the unknown wildflower, and find a match by comparing your seed head to the seed heads in the drawings at the beginning of each section. If you can't decide which seed-head category to choose, pick the two most likely and go through the species descriptions in each category.

Once you have chosen a seed-head category, match your unknown plant to the In Seed species descriptions for this category. You will need to observe other characteristics on the stalk and seed head, such as leaves, hair, odor, and stalk shape.

Many plants still have green leaves or intact dormant leaves on the plant when seeds begin to ripen. Leaf characteristics such as shape, margins, and connection to and arrangement on the stalk can be used to identify the plant; see the drawings at the back of the book for examples. Use leaf texture (rough when rubbed), hair on the stalk and/or leaves, and stalk shape (square, winged, incised) to assist you. All these terms are clearly defined in the glossary to help you.

Some early-season flowering species such as prairie phlox, shooting star, prairie violet, and prairie smoke are small-stature plants easily lost in the taller vegetation in early summer when their seeds are ripe. Whenever possible, mark these plants with field flags or use a GPS app on your smartphone when they are in flower so you can find them later to collect seeds. Each of these low-stature plants is denoted by a flag icon on its species description page.

How Many Seeds Can I Expect from Each Plant?

The number of seeds produced by a prairie plant varies greatly by species. Some plants, like tall cinquefoil, produce thousands of seeds on a single plant, while others, like hairy puccoon, may have fewer than ten seeds. In addition, a plant may appear to have a great number of seeds but have only a few filled seeds inside once the seed head is opened. Seed production for each species has been categorized as "very few," "few," "moderate," or "high" in the descriptions to guide you. See table 3 for a list of the number of seeds produced per stalk for each species in this book.

How Do I Know When Seeds Are Ripe for a Given Species?

In addition to the date given in each description, tables 1 and 2 list the initial ripening time for each species. Keep in mind that these dates are approximate and can vary by a few weeks. The easiest way to assess if seeds are ripe is to pick a seed and try to dent it with your fingernail. Ripe seeds will not dent.

How Long Will the Seeds Remain on the Plant?

Plants hold their seeds for various times from a day or two after ripening (e.g., prairie violet) to well into late winter (e.g., wild petunia). Given average climatic conditions for a particular location, most species included in this book can hold the majority of their seeds for up to a month after ripening. After that time, dry and/or windy conditions will accelerate seed loss off the stalk. Table 2 also lists the approximate length of time that seeds will hold on to each plant after ripening.

How Do I Collect the Seeds?

There are many different ways to collect seeds, from hand-harvesting to machine-harvesting with a combine. The focus of this book, however, is on hand-harvesting. Many seed heads can be simply broken off the stalk by hand, put into a container, and cleaned later. Some species, such as purple and white prairie clover, can be

Hardware wire screens (at ends) and brass soil sieves (center) used to hand-clean prairie seeds. Wood frames are constructed around hardware screens (¼-inch and ⅛-inch openings) to be nested and fit snugly on an 18-gallon storage tub for screening larger quantities of seeds. For screening smaller quantities, a soil sieve (center) can be used.

peeled off the stalk. Seed heads of some species, such as prairie coreopsis and pale purple coneflower, need to be cut from the stalk with scissors because their heads are held very tightly and will not break off the stalk by hand.

Why and How Do I Clean the Seeds?

Cleaning seeds is the process of breaking down a seed head containing many seeds and nonseed parts into individual seeds and removing the nonseed parts. Cleaning the seeds gives you a better idea of how many seeds were collected but does not indicate seed viability, the actual quantity of live seeds. To determine seed viability, a subsample of the collected seeds would need to be sent to a seed-testing laboratory such as Hulsey Seed Laboratory for a germination viability test.

Once you have collected seeds in the field, follow the specific recommendations for seed cleaning in the Seed Harvesting section for that species. Most species included in this book can be cleaned by stomping, screening, and/or sifting.

How Do I Store Seeds?

Prairie seed viability greatly decreases with increasing temperature and humidity. The general rule for seed storage is that temperature plus relative humidity should not exceed 100 where the seeds are stored. Most prairie seeds will last up to a year if stored at 50°F with 50 percent relative humidity. The best place to store seeds is in the refrigerator until you plant them.

Allium canadense, wild garlic
Anemone canadensis, Canada anemone
Echinacea pallida, pale purple coneflower
Heliopsis helianthoides, ox-eye sunflower
Monarda fistulosa, wild bergamot
Rudbeckia hirta, black-eyed Susan

Anemone cylindrica, thimbleweed
Coreopsis palmata, prairie coreopsis
Dalea candida, white prairie clover
Ratibida pinnata, gray-headed coneflower

PART ONE
Solitary Seed Heads

Dalea purpurea, purple prairie clover
Helianthus pauciflorus, prairie sunflower

Geum triflorum, prairie smoke

Viola pedatifida, prairie violet

1 *Allium canadense*, wild garlic
Liliaceae, lily family

SEED PRODUCTION ▸ very few bulbs, very few seeds
SEED DURATION ▸ short

IN FLOWER Flowering begins in early June. On flowering plants, the inflorescence is a round umbel that consists of many small ½-inch-wide pink to white flowers with six tepals. Flowers on most plants may be partially or entirely replaced by bulblets. Bulblets can be planted directly in the soil. Found in wet-mesic, mesic, and dry-mesic soils in full sunlight and partial shade. This species should be marked with field flags while in flower to ensure it can be found for seed harvesting.

IN SEED Plants are 1 to 2 feet tall. If the plant produces seeds, look down for a round umbel-shaped seed head with a small capsule at each stem tip, containing four glossy black seeds (compare wild prairie onion in part 6). If the plant has bulblets, look for a cluster of them
▸ at the terminal end of a short stalk. Stalks with bulblets sometimes lodge over, making it difficult to spot these in the field. Leaves are long, narrow, and dark green and taper to a pointed tip. Leaves appear glossy, without leaf venation, and crushing will produce a strong onion odor. Bulblets are teardrop-shaped and cream-colored and vary in size, averaging about ⁵⁄₁₆ inch (8 mm) wide by ⁵⁄₁₆ inch (8 mm) long.

SEED HARVESTING Ripening begins in early July. Each stalk will produce very few bulblets or few seeds, and both are easily removed by hand-harvesting. Don't pick unripe bulblets or seeds when green; wait till the bulblets turn a cream color or capsules are open, exposing black seeds, to ensure for ripeness. Monitor the plants closely because bulblets and seeds shatter readily from the stalk near ripening time.

Anemone canadensis, Canada anemone
Ranunculaceae, buttercup family

SEED PRODUCTION ▸ very few
SEED DURATION ▸ short

IN FLOWER Flowering begins in late May. The inflorescence is terminal and solitary, consisting of one or a few medium-size five-petaled white flowers with a yellow center up to 1 ¾ inches wide. Found in wet-mesic and mesic soils in full sunlight and partial shade.

IN SEED Plants are only about 1 foot tall. Look down for a large patch of low-growing green leaves oriented horizontally, facing the sky. Emanating from the center of the leaves is a terminal sphere-shaped seed mass ▸ connected to a short stem. The sphere consists of individual tightly packed seeds. Each seed has a pointed tail that faces outward. Leaves are deeply lobed with three distinct sections and serrate margins and are connected to a petiole that emanates from the ground. Seeds are 9⁄32 inch (7 mm) long, dark brown or yellowish-green, and ovate with a pointed tail at the wide end.

SEED HARVESTING Ripening begins in late July. Each stalk produces very few seeds. As the seeds ripen, the sphere turns from light green to mottled yellow-brown to completely brown. Collect seeds when the sphere is yellow-brown; waiting until the sphere is brown may be too late, as seeds quickly shatter. It is easy to harvest seeds by hand-pulling. Gently place the yellow-brown mottled sphere between your fingers in the palm of your hand and pull upward. The seed sphere will completely shatter into your hand, leaving only individual seeds. No further seed cleaning is needed.

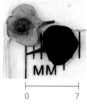

MM

0   7

Anemone cylindrica, thimbleweed
Ranunculaceae, buttercup family

SEED PRODUCTION ▸ moderate
SEED DURATION ▸ medium

IN FLOWER Flowering begins in late June. The inflorescence is terminal and solitary, consisting of one or a few small white flowers ¾ inch across with five pointed petals and a green raised center up to 1 ¼ inches long. Petals drop off soon after flowering; thus, this plant is sometimes called windflower. Found in dry-mesic and dry soils in full sunlight.

IN SEED Plants are 1 ½ to 2 ½ feet tall. Look for a foliated stalk with a terminal thimble-shaped seed head connected to a long, leafless, hairy stem. The seed head is ⅜ inch wide and 1 ¼ inches long. Some yellow and brown lower leaves may remain on the stalk when the seeds are ripe. Leaves have three distinct lobes with serrate margins and are connected by a short petiole. After ripening, the seed head loses its shape ▸ and becomes what looks like a cotton ball. Other thimbleweed plants are likely present in the area. Seeds are ⅛ inch (3 mm) long, ovate, with a short tail on the wide end and light or dark brown in color.

SEED HARVESTING Ripening begins in early August. This species produces moderate numbers of seeds. Determining seed ripeness is difficult, since a ripe (but intact) seed head looks identical to an unripe seed head. To ensure the seeds are ripe, check the peduncle; if it is brown, then the seeds are ready to harvest. Ripe seeds and cotton will pull easily off the peduncle. Thimbleweed seeds can remain into late summer as a cottony mass, but one strong wind will end seed harvesting for this species.

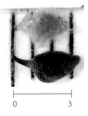

0   3

Coreopsis palmata, prairie coreopsis
Asteraceae, daisy family

SEED PRODUCTION ▸ few
SEED DURATION ▸ long

IN FLOWER Flowering begins in mid-June. The inflorescence is terminal and solitary, consisting of one or a few yellow daisy-shaped flower heads with a yellow center. Found in mesic, dry-mesic, and dry soils in full sunlight and partial shade.

IN SEED Plants are 1½ to 2½ feet tall. Look for a large patch of plants containing many stalks. Each stalk typically has a terminal, solitary, kettle-shaped dark brown to black seed head. The patch will be dense enough to reduce growth of other plant species and is easily seen in the field. After a hard frost the entire plant, including leaves, turns black, making the patch even more visible. Leaves remain connected to the stalk when the seeds are ripe. ▸ Leaves have three distinctive elongated strap-like lobes, are sessile, and are arranged opposite on the stalk. Seeds are 3/16 inch (5 mm) long, oval, flattened, and dark brown.

SEED HARVESTING Ripening begins in mid-September. Each stalk produces few seeds. The dried seed head holds very tightly to the stem and must be cut from the stalk to harvest the seeds. Seed heads with seeds will remain on the stalk well into fall. Seed heads remain hard after harvesting and need physical crushing to extract the seeds. Stomp heads and stems in a utility tub to crush the seed heads. Sift the material through ⅛-inch-opening wire screen to separate out the seeds.

MM

0   5

Dalea candida, white prairie clover
Fabaceae, legume family

SEED PRODUCTION ▸ moderate
SEED DURATION ▸ long

IN FLOWER Flowering begins in early July. The inflorescence is a cylindrical spike head of white flowers. Each head consists of numerous pea-shaped flowers, 1/16 inch wide, arranged like a collar around each elongated flower head. Found in mesic, dry-mesic, and dry soils in full sunlight and partial shade.

IN SEED Plants are 1 ½ to 3 feet tall. Look within drier areas of the grass canopy for a foliated stalk with a solitary or a few terminal dark brown or black cylindrical seed heads ⅜ inch wide and up to 1 ½ inches long. ▸ Sticking out from the seed head will be short string-like hair. Some lower leaves on the stalk may remain connected when seeds are ripe. Leaves are odd-pinnately compound with five or seven strap-shaped leaflets and are arranged alternately on the stalk. Other plants of this species may be found closeby. Seeds are 1/16 inch (2 mm) long, oval, and tan.

SEED HARVESTING Ripening begins in late September. Each stalk produces moderate numbers of seeds. While seeds can be easily stripped off by hand-pulling, don't assume that there are a lot of seeds present. White prairie clover seeds are covered by a fibrous husk. Many of the husks will not be filled with seeds, so it is important to periodically check for seeds when harvesting. Rub a few seeds between your fingers to remove the husk and expose the seeds inside. No further cleaning is needed. Seeds can remain on the stalk into late fall.

0   4

Dalea purpurea, purple prairie clover
Fabaceae, legume family

SEED PRODUCTION ▸ moderate
SEED DURATION ▸ long

IN FLOWER Flowering begins in early July. The inflorescence is a cylindrical spike head of purple flowers. Each head consists of numerous pea-shaped flowers, ¹⁄₁₆ inch wide, arranged like a collar around each elongated flower head. Found in mesic, dry-mesic, and dry soils in full sunlight and partial shade.

IN SEED Plants are 1 ½ to 3 feet tall. Look within drier areas of the grass canopy for a foliated stalk with a solitary or a few terminal ashy-gray cylindrical seed heads ½ inch wide by up to 1 ½ inches long. Some green lower leaves may still be connected to the stalk when seeds are ripe. Leaves are odd-pinnately compound with three or five strap-shaped leaflets and are arranged alternately on the stalk. Green leaves have a citrus odor when crushed. Other plants of this species may be found closeby. Seeds are ¹⁄₁₆ inch (2 mm) long, oval, and tan.

SEED HARVESTING Ripening begins in late September. Each stalk produces moderate numbers of seeds. Purple prairie clover seeds are covered by a soft and hairy husk. While seeds can be easily stripped off by hand-pulling, don't assume that there are seeds present. Many of the husks will not be filled with seeds, so it is important to periodically check for seeds when harvesting. Rub a few seeds between your fingers to remove the husk and expose the seeds inside. No further cleaning is needed. Seeds can remain on the stalk into late fall.

0   3

Echinacea pallida, pale purple coneflower
Asteraceae, daisy family

SEED PRODUCTION ▸ moderate
SEED DURATION ▸ long

IN FLOWER Flowering begins in mid-June. The inflorescence is terminal and solitary, consisting of one or a few large flower heads up to 3 inches wide, with light purple to pinkish-purple drooping rays and a dark dome-shaped center. Found in mesic, dry-mesic, and dry soils in full sunlight.

IN SEED Plants are 2 to 3 feet tall. Look for a stalk that is nearly black in color with a terminal, solitary dome-shaped black and prickly seed head 1 inch wide by 1 inch long. Any leaves remaining on the stalk will be shriveled and unidentifiable, but some green and yellow basal leaves may be present when seeds are ripe. Basal leaves are lance-shaped and connect to a long petiole that emanates from the plant crown at ground level. Coarse short hair covers the entire plant, feeling rough to the touch. Seeds are ¼ inch (6 mm) long with the husk intact and tan and brown in color.

SEED HARVESTING Ripening begins in late September. Each stalk produces moderate numbers of seeds. Cut seed heads off the stalk. Gloves should be worn when harvesting the seeds because prickly heads will puncture bare skin. Stomp heads and stems in a utility tub to release seeds. Then sift the crushed material through ⅛-inch-opening hardware screen to separate out the seeds. Seed heads remain connected to the stalk into winter, but seeds eventually shatter out of the head, so check for seeds if harvesting later in the season.

0   6

⌐ *Geum triflorum*, prairie smoke
Rosaceae, rose family

SEED PRODUCTION ▸ very few
SEED DURATION ▸ short

IN FLOWER Flowering begins in early May. The inflorescence is terminal and solitary, consisting of a few nodding red flowers connected to a leafless peduncle. Each flower has a closed sepal head (calyx) and long, narrow red bracts that radiate from the base. Found in wet-mesic, mesic, and dry-mesic soils in full sunlight and partial shade. This species should be marked with field flags while in flower to ensure it can be found for seed harvesting.

IN SEED Plants are 6 inches to 1 foot tall. Look down into the vegetation for a few terminal white cottony, thread-like masses connected to a short, leafless, hairy stem. The thread-like masses are actually hairy styles connected to seeds in the head. Leaves are green when seeds are ripe. ▸ Directly around the flower stalk and close to the ground will be a rosette of pinnately divided leaves that connect to a petiole emanating from the crown of the plant. Seeds are 1/16 inch (2 mm) long, teardrop-shaped, and brown, with a hairy style up to 1 ½ inches in length.

SEED HARVESTING Ripening begins in mid-June. Each stalk produces very few seeds. Tan sepals and bracts at the base of the seed head indicate the seeds are ripe. Seeds can be easily harvested by hand but also easily shatter soon after ripening, so don't expect to collect a lot of seeds of this species. Best advice is to monitor the marked plants near ripening time so as not to miss the harvest window.

Helianthus pauciflorus, prairie sunflower
Asteraceae, daisy family

SEED PRODUCTION ▸ very few
SEED DURATION ▸ long

IN FLOWER Flowering begins in early August. The inflorescence is terminal and solitary, with daisy-shaped flowers with yellow rays and dark brown centers. Found in wet-mesic, mesic, dry-mesic, and dry soils in full sunlight.

IN SEED Plants are 3 to 4 feet tall. Look in drier areas for a foliated stalk, with one or a few terminal brown seed heads. Some stalks may have terminal seed heads on branched stem tips. ▸ This species is easier to identify in the field than other sunflowers because it has long stems and widely spaced leaf pairs. Leaves are elongated and oval and taper to a tip, with finely serrate margins and a prominent midvein. Leaves on the upper portion of the stalk are sessile and arranged opposite. Stalk and leaves feel very rough when rubbed. It is likely that many other plants of this species will be found in the same area. Seeds are ³⁄₁₆ inch (5 mm) long, oval, tapered at one end, and brown.

SEED HARVESTING Ripening begins in late September. Each stalk produces very few seeds. Seeds are ripe when the seed head is brown. Cut seed heads off the stalk when harvesting. Periodically check for seeds by crushing the head in your hand to extract them. Seed heads remain intact after harvesting. Stomp seed heads and stems in a utility tub to dislodge the seeds. Sift crushed material through ⅛-inch-opening wire screen to separate out the seeds. Seed heads remain on the stalk into late fall.

MM

0   5

Heliopsis helianthoides, ox-eye sunflower
Asteraceae, daisy family

SEED PRODUCTION ▸ moderate
SEED DURATION ▸ long

IN FLOWER Flowering begins in mid-June and continues into late July. The inflorescence is terminal and solitary, with daisy-shaped flower heads with yellow rays and gold disk centers. Found in wet-mesic, mesic, and dry-mesic soils in full sunlight and partial shade.

IN SEED Plants are 3 to 4 feet tall. Look for a foliated stalk with one or a few terminal dark brown or black seed heads. Leaves are ovate, taper to a point, and have serrate margins. Leaves are attached to the stalk with a short petiole and are arranged opposite. Very short coarse hair can be seen on the stalk and leaves and will feel rough when rubbed. Seeds are ⁵⁄₃₂ inch (4 mm) long, oval, tapering at one end, slightly curved, and dark brown.

SEED HARVESTING Ripening begins in late September. Each stalk produces moderate numbers of seeds. Plants of this species flower over many weeks, and there may be differential ripening among plants. It is important to check for seed ripeness when harvesting. Seeds are ripe if the seed head is brown; leave green or yellow heads on the stalk to further ripen. Cut seed heads off the main stalk when harvesting. Stomp seed heads and stems in a utility tub to dislodge the seed. Sift crushed material through ⅛-inch-opening wire screen to separate out the seeds. Seed heads remain on the stalk into late fall.

MM

0   4

Monarda fistulosa, wild bergamot
Lamiaceae, mint family

SEED PRODUCTION ▸ high
SEED DURATION ▸ long

IN FLOWER Flowering begins in mid-July. The inflorescence is terminal and solitary, with pink to light purple flower heads. Each flower head has numerous tube-shaped, two-lobed flowers. Found in wet-mesic, mesic, dry-mesic, and dry soils in full sunlight and partial shade.

IN SEED Plants are 2 to 4 feet tall. Look for a foliated stalk with one or a few terminal whitish-brown, dome-shaped seed heads, approximately ¾ inch wide. Each seed head consists of numerous upright tubes that feel soft to the touch and release a mint odor when rubbed. ▸ The stalk has a square stem. Leaves are lance-shaped with pointed tips and serrate margins and are arranged opposite on the stalk. Seeds are ¹⁄₁₆ inch (2 mm) long, dark brown, and oval.

SEED HARVESTING Ripening begins in late September. Each stalk produces high numbers of seeds. Seed heads will be brown when the seeds are ripe and can be easily broken from the stalk. Vigorously rub seed heads and stems against ¼-inch-opening hardware screen placed over a utility tub to dislodge seeds from the seed heads. Then sift the tub material through a standard 18-mesh screen sieve to separate out the seeds. Seed heads remain on the stalk into late fall.

0   2

Ratibida pinnata, gray-headed coneflower
Asteraceae, daisy family

SEED PRODUCTION ▸ high
SEED DURATION ▸ long

IN FLOWER Flowering begins in mid-July. The inflorescence is terminal and solitary, with long-stemmed flower heads with yellow drooping petals and a raised, dark brown dome-shaped center. Found in mesic and dry-mesic soils in full sunlight and partial shade.

IN SEED Plants are 3 to 5 feet tall. Look for a foliated stalk with a few terminal grayish-brown, thimble-shaped seed heads connected to long branched stems. ▸ Each seed head is ½ inch wide by ⅞ inch long and covered with small brown dots. Some lower leaves on the stalk will remain when seeds are ripe. Leaves are compound with highly dissected leaf lobes and are arranged alternately on the stalk. Much larger leaves of a similar shape with long petioles emanate from the crown of the plant near the ground. Seeds are ⅛ inch (3 mm) long, black, and oval with four distinct ridges running along their length.

SEED HARVESTING Ripening begins in mid-September. Each stalk produces high numbers of seeds. Seeds are ripe when the seed head turns grayish-brown. Seed heads hold tightly to the stem and will need to be broken off or cut when harvesting. Harvesting seeds of this species will produce a strong odor of black licorice. Vigorously stomp seed heads and stems in a utility tub to break apart the seed heads. Sift the crushed material through a standard 14-mesh screen sieve to separate out the seeds. Seed heads remain on the stalk into late fall.

Rudbeckia hirta, black-eyed Susan
Asteraceae, daisy family

SEED PRODUCTION ▸ high
SEED DURATION ▸ long

IN FLOWER Flowering begins in early July. The inflorescence is terminal and solitary, with long-stemmed daisy-shaped flowers with yellow rays and a dark brown dome-shaped center. Found in mesic, dry-mesic, and dry soils in full sunlight and partial shade.

IN SEED Plants are 1 to 2 feet tall. Look for an upright brown or black stalk consisting of one or a few terminal and brown dome-shaped seed heads. Each head is connected to a branched stem tip. ▸ All parts of the plant are covered in fuzzy hair. Leaves still attached to the stalk when seeds are ripe will be brown, shriveled, and unidentifiable. This species has an identifiable rosette of leaves at the base of the stalk. Basal leaves are lance- and ovate-shaped with irregular serrate margins, connected to a long petiole, and are very hairy. Seeds are 1/16 inch (2 mm) long, black, rod-shaped, and slightly curved.

SEED HARVESTING Ripening begins in late September. Each stalk produces high numbers of seeds. The seeds are ripe when seed heads turn brown. Cut seed heads off the stalk when harvesting. Seed heads remain on the stalks well into fall but may have shattered their seeds. Periodically crush the seed head in your palm to check for seeds if harvesting later in the season. Vigorously rub seed heads and stems against 1/8-inch-opening hardware screen placed over a utility tub to dislodge seeds from the heads. Sift the material through a standard 14-mesh screen sieve to separate out the seeds.

0   2

Viola pedatifida, prairie violet
Violaceae, violet family

SEED PRODUCTION ▸ few
SEED DURATION ▸ very short

IN FLOWER Flowering begins in early May. The inflorescence is solitary, consisting of a few blue to violet five-petaled flowers nodding on short peduncles. Found in mesic, dry-mesic, and dry soils in full sunlight and partial shade. This species should be marked with field flags while in flower to ensure it can be found for seed harvesting.

IN SEED Plants are up to 6 inches tall. Look down near the ground for a green rosette of basal leaves consisting of deeply lobed leaves with long petioles, connected to the plant crown on the ground. ▸ Expect to find only a few nodding, oval capsules terminally connected to short leafless stems in the basal leaf rosette. Capsules are ⅝ inch long by ¼ inch wide. Seeds are ¹⁄₁₆ inch (2 mm) long, hard, and brown with a teardrop shape.

SEED HARVESTING Ripening begins in mid-June. This species produces few seeds. It is very difficult to collect seeds from prairie violet. Capsules open within days after ripening, ejecting all their seeds to the ground. ▸ As the capsule ripens, it turns upward on the stalk and should be harvested at this stage before it shatters the seeds. Best chance of collecting seeds is to check capsules daily near the ripening time. This species has cleistogamous flowers that self-fertilize, meaning that some flowers never open and develop into seed-filled capsules. Place harvested capsules in a closed container; within a few days they will rupture and release their seeds.

PART TWO

Seeds in Follicles

Asclepias incarnata, swamp milkweed
Asclepias tuberosa, butterfly milkweed
Asclepias verticillata, whorled milkweed

Asclepias incarnata, swamp milkweed
Asclepiadaceae, milkweed family

SEED PRODUCTION ▸ moderate
SEED DURATION ▸ short

IN FLOWER Flowering begins in early July. The inflorescence consists of many round umbel flower clusters at the terminal end of the stalk. Flowers have unique reflexed petals, pink to red, with a highly aromatic vanilla scent and are utilized by monarch and swallowtail caterpillars. Found in wet-mesic and mesic soils in full sunlight.

IN SEED Plants are up to 5 feet tall. Look in wetter areas for a tall foliated stalk with many upward-pointed follicles 3 inches long and ½ inch wide. Follicles are connected at branched stem tips at the terminal end of the main stalk. Leaves are narrow, up to 6 inches long, arranged opposite on the stalk, and remain connected when the seeds are ripe. Seeds are ³⁄₁₆ inch (5 mm) long, reddish-brown, with a soft membrane around the edges. Other plants of this species are likely to be growing in the same area.

SEED HARVESTING Ripening begins in late September. Each stalk produces moderate numbers of seeds. Seeds are ripe when follicles turn from light green to tan. Before harvesting, gently squeeze a follicle to pop it open (just a little) to ensure seeds are ripe. Ripe seeds should be brown. If seeds are cream-colored, leave the follicle to ripen for another day or two. It is possible to leave the white floss in the follicle while removing seeds, but this must be done within hours after harvesting. Squeeze the follicle near the pointed end and hold the floss firmly between the finger and thumb. With the other hand, gently scrape the seeds from the floss bundle. No additional cleaning is needed.

Asclepias tuberosa, butterfly milkweed
Asclepiadaceae, milkweed family

SEED PRODUCTION ▸ moderate
SEED DURATION ▸ short

IN FLOWER Flowering begins in late June. The inflorescence consists of many umbel flower clusters at the terminal end of the stalk. Flowers are orange to red with unique reflexed petals. Found in mesic, dry-mesic, and dry soils in full sunlight and partial shade.

IN SEED Plants are 2 to 3 feet tall. Look in drier areas for mostly green, slightly bent stalks with many follicles, 4 inches long and ½ inch wide. Follicles point upward near the terminal end of the stalk and are easily seen. Leaves are narrow, up to 4 inches long, arranged alternately on the stalk, and remain intact when the seeds are ripe. Seeds are ¼ inch (6 mm) long, reddish-brown, with a soft membrane around the edges. Leaves and stalk are covered with fine fuzzy hair.

SEED HARVESTING Ripening begins in early September. Each stalk will produce a moderate number of seeds. Follicles typically ripen over a narrow two-week period. Check daily. Pick follicles that are mostly reddish-orange — very similar in color to a ripe peach — and leave green pods to further ripen. Before harvesting, gently squeeze a follicle to pop it open (just a little) to ensure the seeds are ripe. If seeds are cream-colored and not brown, leave the follicle to ripen another day or two. It is possible to leave the white floss in the follicle while removing the seeds, but this must be done within hours after harvesting. Squeeze the follicle near the pointed end and hold the floss firmly between the finger and thumb. With the other hand, gently scrape the seeds from the floss bundle.

MM

0   6

Asclepias verticillata, whorled milkweed
Asclepiadaceae, milkweed family

SEED PRODUCTION ▸ moderate
SEED DURATION ▸ short

IN FLOWER Flowering begins in early July. The inflorescence consists of many small flat umbel clusters on the upper end of the stalk. Individual flowers are small and white, with unique reflexed petals. This species quickly establishes and disappears in disturbed areas. Found in mesic, dry-mesic, and dry soils in full sunlight.

IN SEED Plants are 1 to 2 feet tall. Look in recently disturbed, drier areas for upright foliated stalks with multiple follicles 3 inches long and ¼ inch wide. Follicles point upward and will be located near the terminal end of the stalk. A few green leaves will remain on the stalk until a killing frost and will be sessile, narrow, straplike, and arranged in a whorl. Seeds are ³⁄₁₆ inch (5 mm) long, reddish-brown, with a soft membrane around the edges. This species typically grows in patches consisting of many plants.

SEED HARVESTING Ripening begins in late September. Each stalk will produce a moderate number of seeds. As the seeds ripen, follicles turn from light green to tan. ▸ Before harvesting, gently squeeze a follicle to pop it open (just a little) to ensure seeds are ripe. If seeds are cream-colored and not brown, leave the follicle to ripen another day or two. It is possible to leave the white floss in the follicle while removing the seeds, but this must be done within hours after harvesting. Squeeze the follicle near the pointed end and hold the floss firmly between the finger and thumb. With the other hand, gently scrape the seeds from the floss bundle.

0   5

PART THREE

Seeds in Leaf Axils

Lithospermum caroliniense, hairy puccoon
Onosmodium molle, false gromwell

1 *Lithospermum caroliniense*, hairy puccoon
Boraginaceae, forget-me-not family

SEED PRODUCTION ▸ very few
SEED DURATION ▸ short

IN FLOWER Flowering begins in early June. The inflorescence consists of a terminal cluster of brilliant small orange-yellow, five-lobed, tube-shaped flowers ½ inch wide. Found in dry-mesic and dry soils in full sunlight and partial shade. This species should be marked with field flags while in flower to ensure it can be found for seed harvesting.

IN SEED Plants are 1 to 2 feet tall. Look in very dry areas for a few closely grouped and bent-over green foliated stalks low to the ground. Leaves vary in size on the stalk, consisting of larger stalk leaves and very small narrow sepal leaves. Stalk leaves are oval, up to ⅜ inch wide by 1 ¼ inches long, and taper at the tip. Sepal leaves are strap-shaped, 1/16 inch wide and up to ¼ inch long, connected close to the stalk and arranged in a whorl. Both leaves and stalk are hairy. Seeds are 5/32 inch (4 mm) long, teardrop-shaped, and glossy white.

SEED HARVESTING Ripening begins in late July. This species produces very few seeds. Ripe seeds have a white glossy coat; unripe seeds are green and glossy. ▸ Look for individual shiny white teardrop-shaped seeds nestled in leaf axils, surrounded by five thin leaf-like green hairy bracts close to the stalk. Seeds are easy to hand-pull from the stalk, but expect to find only a few seeds on each stalk. Seeds easily shatter from the stalks soon after ripening, so frequently check the plants.

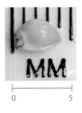

Onosmodium molle, false gromwell
Boraginaceae, forget-me-not family

SEED PRODUCTION ▸ very few
SEED DURATION ▸ short

IN FLOWER Flowering begins in mid-June. The inflorescence is a short terminal raceme of a few tubed-shaped, cream-colored drooping flower heads. Each head has a ¾-inch thread-like style protruding from the end. Found in dry-mesic and dry soils in full sunlight.

IN SEED Plants are 1 to 2 feet tall. Look for a low-growing and foliated shrub-like plant, with a close grouping of drooping bent stalks. All parts of the plant are covered with coarse short hair that is easily seen and will help with identification. Leaves are oval, with prominent parallel veins and hair on the leaf surface, and arranged alternately on the stalk. Individual teardrop-shaped, tan seeds are nestled in leaf axils on the upper part of the stem. Seeds are ⁵⁄₃₂ inch (4 mm) long, white or tan, hard, and glossy.

SEED HARVESTING Ripening begins in early September. Each stalk produces very few seeds. Ripe seeds are white or tan; unripe seeds have various shades of green. Seeds are easily removed by hand-harvesting. Harvesting seeds for this species is difficult because of differential seed ripening. It is common to find seeds in all stages of ripening on the same plant. Seeds also easily shatter from the stalk upon ripening, adding to harvesting challenges. Check plants frequently near ripening time and collect seeds when possible. Consider yourself lucky if you can harvest seeds of this species.

Baptisia alba, white wild indigo
Lobelia siphilitica, great blue lobelia

Baptisia bracteata, cream false indigo

Silphium laciniatum, compass plant

Chamaecrista fasciculata, partridge pea

PART FOUR
Seeds in Racemes

Lespedeza capitata, round-headed bush clover

Ceanothus americanus, New Jersey tea

Delphinium virescens, prairie larkspur

Baptisia alba, white wild indigo
Fabaceae, legume family

SEED PRODUCTION ▸ high
SEED DURATION ▸ long

IN FLOWER Flowering begins in early June. The inflorescence is a terminal raceme of white pea-shaped flowers arranged along a vertical flowering stalk that may reach 6 feet. Found in wet-mesic, mesic, and dry-mesic soils in full sunlight.

IN SEED The plant is 2 to 3 feet tall with a seed stalk up to 6 feet tall. Look for a tall raceme consisting of many large black pods rising above the prairie vegetation. Pods are oval, ½ inch wide and 1 inch long, and have small pointed tips. Leaves are green on the stalk when seeds are ripe and are compound, with three distinct balloon-shaped leaflets, and arranged alternately on the stalk. The entire plant turns black in early fall, making this species very visible against most other prairie plants going into dormancy. Seeds are 5/32 inch (4 mm) long, oval, and light to dark brown in color.

SEED HARVESTING Ripening begins in late September. Each stalk produces high numbers of seeds. As the seeds ripen, the pods turn from green to black. It is best to cut the entire pod stalk off the plant when harvesting. Open pods periodically when harvesting and check for little black bugs with a curved snout or any signs of fungus growth. The wild indigo weevil (*Apion rostrum*) eats this species' seeds and may introduce a fungus that also destroys them (Mundahl and Plucinski 2010). Dark seeds are viable, so don't discard them (Boyle and Hladun 2005). Stomp pods in a utility tub to release seeds from pods. Sift the crushed material through ⅛-inch-opening hardware screen to separate out the seeds.

0   4

Baptisia bracteata, cream false indigo
Fabaceae, legume family

SEED PRODUCTION ▸ high
SEED DURATION ▸ long

IN FLOWER Flowering begins in mid-May. The inflorescence is a horizontal raceme of cream-colored pea-shaped flowers located within the plant canopy near the ground. Found in mesic, dry-mesic, and dry soils in full sunlight and partial shade.

IN SEED Plants are 1½ to 2 feet tall. Look in dry areas for a short, leafy, shrub-like plant. Compound leaves have three distinct balloon-shaped leaflets, arranged alternately on the stalk, and have a distinctive grayish coloration and fine hair. Each flower stalk has multiple oval blackish-gray pods ¾ inch wide and 1½ inches long with a bent pointed tail on the pod end. Pods are located under the leaf canopy of the plant and are not easily seen. Seeds are 5⁄32 inch (4 mm) long, oblanceolate, and light to dark brown.

SEED HARVESTING Ripening begins in mid-September. Each stalk produces high numbers of seeds. As the seeds ripen, the pod will turn from green to black. Locate the plant; then rummage for pod stalks in the duff. You may hear the pods rattle before spotting them. Cut entire pod stalks off the plant and open periodically to check for little black bugs with a curved snout and any signs of fungus growth. The wild indigo weevil (*Apion rostrum*) eats this species' seeds and may introduce a fungus that destroys them (Mundahl and Plucinski 2010). Dark seeds are viable, so don't discard them (Boyle and Hladun 2005). Stomp pods in a utility tub to release the seeds from the pods. Sift the crushed material through ⅛-inch-opening hardware screen to separate out the seeds.

0   5

Ceanothus americanus, New Jersey tea
Rhamnaceae, buckthorn family

SEED PRODUCTION ▸ few
SEED DURATION ▸ medium

IN FLOWER Flowering begins in late June. The inflorescence is a panicle of scattered corymbs consisting of tiny ⅛-inch-wide button-like white flower heads. Found in mesic, dry-mesic, and dry soils in full sunlight and partial shade.

IN SEED Plants are up to 2 feet tall. Look for a small, leafy, shrub-like patch growing low to the ground, identifiable by darker green leaves that appear puckered from deep incised veins on the leaf surface. Leaves are oval with serrate margins. They are arranged alternately on the stalk and remain when the seeds are ripe. Short raceme clusters of black seed capsules are connected to the terminal end of leafless stems. Each capsule contains three dark glossy seeds, one per lobe. In late summer, the black coat weathers away, exposing a tan seed capsule. The hard, shiny seeds are ⅛ inch (3 mm) long, oval, and black or dark brown.

SEED HARVESTING Ripening begins in late August. Each stalk produces few seeds. The capsules will either be black or tan when the seeds are ripe. Leave green capsules on the plant to ripen. Cut capsules from the main stalk to harvest the seeds. Harvest seeds near the ripening time, as this species ejects its seeds not long after ripening. ▸ Ejected seeds leave behind a small flat tan disk on the stalk as evidence the seeds are gone. Lightly rub the capsules in a standard 18-inch mesh screen sieve to separate out the seeds.

0   8

Chamaecrista fasciculata, partridge pea
Fabaceae, legume family

SEED PRODUCTION ▸ moderate
SEED DURATION ▸ medium

IN FLOWER Flowering begins in early July. The inflorescence is a raceme of yellow flowers on the upper half of the stalk. Also called large-flowered sensitive pea because leaflet pairs will slowly fold together when touched (Britton and Brown 1970). Found in mesic, dry-mesic, and dry soils in full sunlight.

IN SEED Plants are 2 to 3 feet tall. Look for a short foliated stalk with a raceme consisting of multiple brown pods connecting to the upper half of the stalk. Each pod is 1 ½ to 2 inches long and ³⁄₁₆ inch wide. Many leaves will be green when seeds are ripe. Compound leaves are even-pinnate with up to thirty leaflets and are arranged alternately on the stalk. Seeds are ³⁄₁₆ inch (5 mm) long, hard, black, and teardrop-shaped. Other plants of this species are likely to be growing in the same area.

SEED HARVESTING Ripening begins in early August. Each stalk produces moderate numbers of seeds. Partridge pea is an annual, so expect to see flowering plants alongside plants in seed. Pods turn from light green to tan as seeds ripen. Shortly after seeds ripen, pods twist on the stalk, open, and release seeds, so harvest timing is critical. Cut stalks off below the pods when most are brown, and spread them out on a tarp to dry. Circulate air over the material with a box fan so seeds don't get moldy. Wait a few days; as the material dries, the seeds will be ejected from the pods. Sift pods and seeds over ¼-inch-opening hardware screen to separate out the seeds.

0   5

Delphinium virescens, prairie larkspur
Ranunculaceae, buttercup family

SEED PRODUCTION ▸ few
SEED DURATION ▸ short

IN FLOWER Flowering begins in mid-June. The inflorescence is a raceme consisting of horn-shaped white flowers, open in the front and tapering to a closed spur in the rear. Found in dry-mesic and dry soils in full sunlight. This species should be marked with field flags while in flower to ensure it can be found for seed harvesting.

IN SEED Plants are 2 to 3 feet tall. Look within the grass canopy for a slightly bent or curved raceme consisting of loose clusters of capsules along the main stalk. Each cluster consists of three to four individual capsules ¼ inch wide by ⅝ inch long and oriented upright. Leaves will have either fallen or shriveled such that they cannot be identified when seeds are ripe. Seeds vary from ¹⁄₁₆ inch (2 mm) to ⅛ inch (3 mm) long and are brown, rectangular, and covered with tiny pointed dimples.

SEED HARVESTING Ripening begins in mid-July. Each plant produces few seeds, and seed production varies from some seeds to no seeds among plants. Ripe capsules have a light tan color and are easy to pick off the stalk. Lightly rub capsules against a standard 12-mesh screen sieve to separate out the seeds. Timely harvest is critical for this species. Capsules split apart and drop seeds, and stalks lodge over soon after ripening. Assess plants frequently near the ripening time so as not to miss the harvest.

0   3

Lespedeza capitata, round-headed bush clover
Fabaceae, legume family

SEED PRODUCTION ▸ few
SEED DURATION ▸ long

IN FLOWER Flowering begins in mid-August. The inflorescence is a raceme consisting of tiny white pea-shaped flowers ¹⁄₁₆ inch wide, located in light green dome-shaped heads. Found in mesic, dry-mesic, and dry soils in full sunlight and partial shade.

IN SEED Plants are 2 to 4 feet tall. Look in drier areas for a dark reddish-brown club-like structure on the end of a stalk. The club-like structure is a short terminal raceme consisting of many smaller reddish-brown bract bundles with pointed tips. The main stalk is often slightly bowed when the seeds are ripe. The stalk is covered with fine hair and is very woody. Nearly all leaves will have dropped off the plant at the onset of seed ripening, but a closer look will reveal two dark thread-like stipules at each leaf scar. Seeds are ⅛ inch (3 mm) long, oval, and somewhat flattened with a brown husk covering.

SEED HARVESTING Ripening begins in late September. Each stalk produces few seeds. To assess for seed ripeness, extract and rub the husk from a seed, revealing a small bean-shaped seed. Attempt to dent the seed with your fingernail. Ripe seeds cannot be dented. Seed heads hold very tightly to the woody stalk and need to be cut when harvesting. Vigorously rubbing seed heads against ¼-inch-opening hardware screen placed over a utility tub will separate out the seeds. Seed heads remain on the stalk into late fall.

0   4

Lobelia siphilitica, great blue lobelia
Campanulaceae, harebell family

SEED PRODUCTION ▸ high
SEED DURATION ▸ long

IN FLOWER Flowering begins in mid-August. The inflorescence is a raceme of blue tube-shaped flowers with three lower lobes and two upper lobes. Found primarily in wet-mesic soils in full sunlight and partial shade.

IN SEED Plants are 1 to 3 feet tall. Look down in low, wet areas in the grass or sedge canopy for foliated, upright tan stalks with a raceme of ▸ teardrop-shaped soft capsules ¼ inch wide by ⅜ inch long, oriented upward at a 60-degree angle from the stalk. Curled and stringy sepals with pointed tips connect at the base of each capsule. Some lower leaves remain on the stalk when seeds are ripe. Leaves are elongated and oval, with serrate margins, and arranged alternately on the stalk. Many plants of this species are likely to be growing in the same area. Seeds are very small—less than ¹⁄₆₄ inch (0.5 mm) long—tan, and oval.

SEED HARVESTING Ripening begins in early October. Each stalk produces high numbers of seeds. Capsules will be tan when the seeds are ripe and can be easily stripped from the stalk by hand-pulling. Lightly rub the harvested material through a standard 30-mesh screen sieve to break capsules apart and separate out the seeds. Capsules remain connected and full of seeds on the stalk into late fall, so there is extra time to harvest the seeds. A small hole in the capsule indicates that the *Cleopmiarus hispidulus* weevil has been eating the seed inside (Anderson 1964).

0   1

Silphium laciniatum, compass plant
Asteraceae, daisy family

SEED PRODUCTION ▸ moderate
SEED DURATION ▸ long

IN FLOWER Flowering begins in early July. The inflorescence is a tall raceme of daisy-shaped flowers up to 4 inches across with yellow rays arranged around a gold disk center. Found in wet-mesic, mesic, dry-mesic, and dry soils in full sunlight and partial shade.

IN SEED Plants are 4 to 6 feet tall. Look for a tall, sparsely foliated stalk covered by coarse hair, with racemes of brown seed heads up to 3 inches long facing outward and away. Large pointed bracts surround the outer part of each seed head and radiate outward. Basal leaves of this species are easily recognized. Leaves are large, up to 2 feet wide by 2 feet high, highly dissected, and connect to long petioles joined to the plant crown near the ground. Short coarse hair covers all parts of this plant and feels rough to the touch. Seeds are ½ inch (13 mm) long, plump, oval, and black.

SEED HARVESTING Ripening begins in mid-September. Each stalk produces moderate numbers of seeds. Harvesting seeds for this species is tricky due to differential ripening on a stalk. ▸ Seeds ripen from the top down on the stalk, so pick brown seed heads and leave ▸ green ones on the stalk to ripen. It will take multiple harvesting trips to collect all the seeds. Stomp seed heads in a utility tub to dislodge the seeds from the heads. Sift the crushed material through ½-inch-opening hardware screen to separate out the seeds.

MM
CM 1

0   12

Teucrium canadense, germander

 Gentiana andrewsii, bottle gentian
Penstemon grandiflorus, large-flowered beardtongue
Ruellia humilis, wild petunia

 Monarda punctata, spotted horsemint

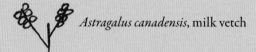 *Astragalus canadensis*, milk vetch

PART FIVE

Seeds in Spikes

Liatris pycnostachya, prairie blazing star

Liatris aspera, rough blazing star

Amorpha canescens, leadplant
Verbena hastata, blue vervain
Verbena stricta, hoary vervain

Amorpha canescens, leadplant
Fabaceae, legume family

SEED PRODUCTION ▸ moderate
SEED DURATION ▸ long

IN FLOWER Flowering begins in late June. The inflorescence consists of densely packed terminal spikes made up of small purple blossoms with distinctive yellow-gold stamens projecting from each flower near the terminal end of the main stalk. Found in mesic, dry-mesic, and dry soils in full sunlight and partial shade.

IN SEED Plants are 1 to 3 feet tall. Look in drier soils for a foliated stalk topped by terminal spikes with dark seedpods covered in a soft husk. Each pod contains a single seed approximately ⅛ inch wide by 3⁄16 inch long, dark-colored, and hairy. Leaves have a distinctive grayish-green color and are odd-pinnately compound, with up to forty-one small oval leaflets arranged alternately on the stalk. All parts of the plant are covered with very fine soft hair. Seeds are 1⁄16 inch (2 mm) long, oval, and vary in color from light green to tan to brown with the husk removed.

SEED HARVESTING Ripening begins in mid-September. Each stalk produces moderate numbers of seeds. Do not use pod color or missing pods on stems to assess for ripeness. Instead, pick a few seeds, rub off the hairy seed coat, and dent the seed with your thumbnail. Ripe seeds will not dent. It is best to cut the entire head off when harvesting. Lightly rub seed heads against ⅛-inch-opening wire screen over a utility tub to separate the seeds from the stems. Pods remain on the stems into late fall.

0   3

Astragalus canadensis, milk vetch
Fabaceae, legume family

SEED PRODUCTION ▸ moderate
SEED DURATION ▸ long

0   5

IN FLOWER Flowering begins in mid-July. The inflorescence is a terminal raceme consisting of densely packed cream and light green tube-shaped flowers. Found in wet-mesic, mesic, and dry-mesic soils in full sunlight and partial shade.

IN SEED Plants are 2 to 3 feet tall. Look for a densely packed spike-like dark brown cluster of smaller pods on leafless stem branches projecting above the foliage. Pods are ³⁄₁₆ inch wide by ½ inch long and oval, with a tail that is slightly tilted at the pod tip. Green leaves are connected to the stalk when seeds are ripe. Leaves are odd-pinnately compound with up to twenty-five oval leaflets and are arranged alternately on the stalk. Seeds are ¹⁄₁₆ inch (2 mm) long, bean-shaped, and light brown.

SEED HARVESTING Ripening begins in mid-September. Each stalk can produce moderate numbers of seeds. Pod clusters need to be cut rather than hand-pulled because they hold tightly to the stem. Periodically check pods to ensure they are filled with healthy seeds. Seeds that are dark and misshapen are most likely not viable. The bruchid beetle larvae eat the seeds of this species. A tiny pinhole in the pod is a clear sign that beetle larvae have been feeding inside the pod (Boe, McDaniel, and Robbins 1989). Pods remain on the stems intact with seeds into late fall. Stomp pods and stems in a utility tub to crush the pods. Sift the material through a standard 14-mesh screen sieve to separate out the seeds. Milk vetch foliage is toxic to humans and mammals if eaten.

Gentiana andrewsii, bottle gentian
Gentianaceae, gentian family

SEED PRODUCTION ▸ high
SEED DURATION ▸ long

IN FLOWER Flowering begins in early September. The inflorescence is a terminal spike of blue flowers with fused petals, forming closed upright blossoms. Flowers are pollinated by bumblebees that claw their way into the closed flower. Found in wet-mesic and mesic soils in full sunlight.

IN SEED Plants are 1 ½ to 2 ½ feet tall. Look in wetter areas for a foliated stalk with a terminal spike of upright capsules on the terminal end of the stalk and in leaf axils below. ▸ Capsules are oval, ⅜ inch wide and 1 inch long, with a short bent tail at the top, and are covered by a papery membrane. Leaves are oval and taper to a pointed tip, are sessile, and arranged opposite on the stalk. It is likely that many other plants of this species will be present in the same area. Seeds are ¹⁄₁₆ inch (2 mm) long, teardrop-shaped, with a dark achene in the center surrounded by a tan membrane.

SEED HARVESTING Ripening begins in mid-October. Each stalk produces high numbers of seeds. Bottle gentian is one of the last wildflower species to flower and to ripen. Capsules have a soft covering and are light tan when ripe. This species should be harvested by cutting off the main stalk below the capsules. Seeds can be extracted by lightly rubbing the capsules against ⅛-inch-opening wire screen placed over a utility tub. Capsules and seeds remain intact on the stalk into late fall.

0   1

Liatris aspera, rough blazing star
Asteraceae, daisy family

SEED PRODUCTION ▸ high
SEED DURATION ▸ long

IN FLOWER Flowering begins in late August. The inflorescence is a raceme of pink to light purple flower heads with short hair-like stamens protruding from center disks closely arranged like buttons on the upper half of the stalk. Found in mesic, dry-mesic, and dry soils in full sunlight.

IN SEED Plants are 2 to 4 feet tall. Look in drier areas for a knee-high foliated stalk with a spike of dome-shaped tan and light purple pappus bristles densely arranged along the upper half of the stalk. Leaves are strap-shaped with a single prominent midvein. They have a very short petiole and are arranged alternately on the stalk. Leaves increase in length down the stalk. Seeds are 3/16 inch (5 mm) long, lance-shaped, with a whitish-tan tuft of pappus bristles connected to the wide end.

SEED HARVESTING Ripening begins in early October. Each stalk produces high numbers of seeds. Seeds ripen on the stalk from the top down. This species sets seeds late; assessing for seed ripeness is important before harvesting. Pappus bristles should be fully extended to a dome shape and should peel easily off the stem when seeds are ripe. Bracts and small stems on the stalk can be abrasive on bare skin, so it's a good idea to wear gloves. Pulling too hard on the stalk while harvesting seeds will damage the plant. The stalk is connected to a corm just below the soil surface and can pop out of the ground.

0   8

Liatris pycnostachya, prairie blazing star
Asteraceae, daisy family

SEED PRODUCTION ▸ high
SEED DURATION ▸ medium

IN FLOWER Flowering begins in late July. The inflorescence is a spike of pink to light purple flower heads with short hair-like stamens protruding outward from the center disk and arranged on the upper half of the stalk. Found in wet-mesic and mesic soils in full sunlight.

IN SEED Plants are 2 ½ to 4 feet tall. Look in wet areas for a foliated stalk with a fuzzy spike of densely packed tan and brown pappus bristles. Each spike is 1 inch wide by 5 to 10 inches long on the upper third of the stalk. Leaves are strap-shaped with a single prominent midvein with a very short petiole. Leaves are arranged alternately and increase in length down the stalk. Seeds are ³⁄₁₆ inch (5 mm) long and lance-shaped, with a whitish tan tuft of pappus bristles connected to the wide end.

SEED HARVESTING Ripening begins in late September. Each stalk produces high numbers of seeds. Seeds ripen on the stalk from the top down so should be assessed for ripeness before harvesting. Fluffed-out pappus bristles visible on each seed head indicate that the seeds are ripe. Seeds are easy to hand-pull from the stalk, but the stalk can be somewhat abrasive on bare skin. Pulling too hard on the stalk while harvesting seeds will damage the plant. The stalk is connected to a corm just below the soil surface and can pop out of the ground.

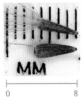

MM

0   8

Monarda punctata, spotted horsemint
Lamiaceae, mint family

SEED PRODUCTION ▸ high
SEED DURATION ▸ long

IN FLOWER Flowering begins in mid-July. The inflorescence is a spike of green and cream flower heads whorled around the main stalk. Each flower head has numerous tube-shaped green flowers with a few cream-colored two-lobed flowers attached. More easily seen in the field are the large pinkish to purple and cream-colored leaf-like sepals that radiate out from the base of each flower head. Found in dry-mesic and dry soils in full sunlight.

IN SEED Plants are 1 ½ to 2 ½ feet tall. Look in very dry or recently disturbed areas for a leafless dark brown stalk with a spike of dome-shaped ⅝-inch-wide seed heads whorled on the main stalk. Each seed head consists of numerous upright tubes that feel soft to the touch and release a mint odor when rubbed. Many short green basal shoots may be seen around the stalk when the plant is in seed. Seeds are ⅟₃₂ inch (1 mm) long, dark brown, and oval.

SEED HARVESTING Ripening begins in late September. Each stalk produces high numbers of seeds. Seed heads will be brown when the seeds are ripe. Cut seed heads off the main stalk when harvesting seeds. Vigorously rub seed heads and stems against ⅛-inch-opening hardware screen placed over a utility tub to dislodge the seeds from the seed head. Sift the tub material through a standard 18-mesh screen sieve to separate out the seeds. Seed heads remain on the stalk into late fall.

Penstemon grandiflorus, large-flowered beardtongue
Scrophulariaceae, figwort family

SEED PRODUCTION ▸ high
SEED DURATION ▸ long

· ·

IN FLOWER Flowering begins in early June. The inflorescence is a spike of white to light pink tube-shaped flowers, whorled around the main stalk. Each flower has three lower and two upper lobes. Found in dry-mesic and dry soils in full sunlight.

IN SEED Plants are 2 to 3 feet tall. Look for knee-high foliated stalks with a spike of hardened teardrop-shaped capsules 1 inch wide by 1 inch long whorled on the stalk. Each whorled cluster can have up to six capsules. The wide end of each capsule connects close to the main stalk, and the narrow ends point upward. Leaves are wide and oval, sessile, and arranged opposite on the stalk. Leaves have a prominent midvein and feel like smooth leather when rubbed. Many plants of this species are likely to be growing in the same area. Seeds are ⅛ inch (3 mm) long, dark brown, with an uneven rectangular shape.

SEED HARVESTING Ripening begins in mid-August. Each stalk produces high numbers of seeds. Capsules turn from light green to brown when ripe. Cut all the capsules off the main stalk when harvesting. Wear gloves as capsule tips have sharp points that will puncture skin. Crushing the capsules is necessary to release the seeds. Vigorously stomp capsules and stems in a utility tub to crush the capsules. Sift the crushed material through a standard 10-mesh screen sieve to separate out the seeds. Capsules remain mostly closed and retain seeds into late summer.

0   3

Ruellia humilis, wild petunia
Acanthaceae, acanthus family

SEED PRODUCTION ▸ few
SEED DURATION ▸ long

IN FLOWER Flowering begins in mid-July. The inflorescence is solitary in leaf axils consisting of a few light purple to violet-blue five-lobed, funnel-shaped flowers located near the middle of the stalk. Found in dry-mesic and dry soils in full sunlight. This species should be marked with field flags while in flower to ensure it can be found for seed harvesting.

IN SEED Plants are ½ to 1 ½ feet tall. Focus on rocky and sandy dry areas of the site to locate this species. Look close to the ground for a hairy, upright leafless stalk with a spike of tan, teardrop-shaped, hard capsules ⅛ inch wide by ⅜ inch long. Capsules are arranged in whorled groups up the stalk. ▸ Sepals are long and twisted, hairy and thread-like, emanating from the base of each capsule, giving the stalk a whitish sheen that makes it more visible in the field. Seeds are ⁵⁄₃₂ inch (4 mm) in diameter, reddish-brown, and nearly circular with a raised bump in the center.

SEED HARVESTING Ripening begins in early October. With numerous capsules on each stalk, this plant appears to produce a lot of seeds, but each capsule contains only four seeds. Seeds are ripe when capsules turn tan or brown and must be cut at the stalk to harvest. No further seed cleaning is needed; just leave capsules in a warm room in a closed bag for a few days and they will explode, ejecting their seeds. Capsules remain intact and full of seeds into winter.

Teucrium canadense, germander
Lamiaceae, mint family

SEED PRODUCTION ▸ few
SEED DURATION ▸ long

IN FLOWER Flowering begins in early July. The inflorescence is a terminal raceme of small pink and white tube-shaped flowers ⅛ inch wide, with one large downward-bent lower lobe and two small side lobes. Found in mesic soils in full sunlight and partial shade.

IN SEED Plants are 2 to 3 feet tall. Look for an upright green foliated stalk with a terminal spike consisting of small open capsules ⅛ inch wide. Leaves are oval, taper to a pointed tip with serrate margins, and are arranged opposite on the stalk. Venation on the leaf surface appears puckered. ▸ The stalk is square with a groove in the middle of each side that extends down the length. Seeds are 1/16 inch (2 mm) long, brown, and dome-shaped with a flat bottom. Small visible dimples cover the surface of each seed.

SEED HARVESTING Ripening begins in mid-September. Each stalk produces few seeds. A single capsule contains only four seeds. Seeds are ripe when capsules have a light tan color and can be easily peeled off the stalk by hand. When harvesting this species, don't be fooled into thinking the seeds have already shattered from the plant just because the capsules have a large open end. Seeds are tucked up into the back of the capsules and are difficult to see. Lightly rub capsules in a 10-mesh screen sieve to separate out the seeds. This species holds most capsules with seeds into late fall.

0 3

Verbena hastata, blue vervain
Verbenaceae, vervain family

SEED PRODUCTION ▸ high
SEED DURATION ▸ long

0   3

IN FLOWER Flowering begins in early July. The inflorescence is a terminal spike of blue tube-shaped flowers with lobes ⅛ inch wide. Found in wet-mesic and mesic soils in full sunlight and partial shade.

IN SEED Plants are 3 to 5 feet tall. Look in wetter soils for a tall green foliated square stalk with a few spiked seed heads. Each spike is made up of numerous tiny hard capsules ½₂ inch wide by ⅛ inch long and can be up to 6 inches long. Upper leaves on the stalk remain intact. Leaves are elongated and oval, with serrate margins, and arranged opposite on the stalk. Many plants of this species are likely to be growing in the same area. Seeds are ¹⁄₁₆ inch (2 mm) long, brown on one side and whitish on the other, with an oval shape and flattened ends.

SEED HARVESTING Ripening begins in late September. Each stalk produces high numbers of seeds. Seeds are ripe when the capsules turn light brown. Cut the entire spike off the stalk below the capsules to harvest the seeds. Vigorously rub seed heads and stems against ⅛-inch-opening hardware screen over a utility tub to separate the seeds from the capsules. Sift the tub material through a standard 20-mesh screen sieve to separate out the seeds. Capsules and seeds remain on the stalk into late fall.

Verbena stricta, hoary vervain
Verbenaceae, vervain family

SEED PRODUCTION ▸ moderate
SEED DURATION ▸ long

IN FLOWER Flowering begins in late June. The inflorescence is a terminal spike of blue tube-shaped flowers with lobes ¼ inch wide. Found in dry-mesic and dry soils in full sunlight and partial shade.

IN SEED Plants are 1 ½ to 3 feet tall. Look in drier, recently disturbed areas within the vegetation for a partially green foliated stalk with a few spikes. Each spike consists of numerous tiny hard capsules ⅛ inch wide by ³⁄₁₆ inch long and can be up to 6 inches long. Some upper leaves on the stalk remain intact. Leaves are oval with serrate margins and arranged opposite on the stalk. Fine fuzzy hair covers the entire plant. Many plants of this species are likely to be growing in the same area. Seeds are ⅛ inch (3 mm) long, brown on one side and whitish on the other, with an oval shape and flattened ends.

SEED HARVESTING Ripening begins in late September. Each stalk produces moderate numbers of seeds. Seeds are ripe when capsules turn light brown. Cut the entire spike off the stalk below the capsules to harvest the seeds. Vigorously rub seed heads and stems against ⅛-inch-opening hardware screen over a utility tub to separate seeds from capsules. Sift the tub material through a standard 20-mesh screen sieve to separate out the seeds. Capsules and seeds remain on the stalk into late fall.

Eryngium yuccifolium,
rattlesnake master

 Dodecatheon meadia,
shooting star

 Allium stellatum,
wild prairie onion

 Lilium michiganense,
Michigan lily

Tradescantia bracteata, prairie spiderwort
Tradescantia ohiensis, Ohio spiderwort

PART SIX

Seeds in Umbels

Euphorbia corollata, flowering spurge
Zizia aurea, golden alexanders

Veronicastrum virginicum,
Culver's root

Silphium integrifolium,
rosinweed

Pycnanthemum pilosum, hairy mountain mint
Pycnanthemum tenuifolium, slender mountain mint
Pycnanthemum virginianum, common mountain mint

Allium stellatum, wild prairie onion
Liliaceae, lily family

SEED PRODUCTION ▸ few
SEED DURATION ▸ short

IN FLOWER Flowering begins in early August. The inflorescence is a round umbel that consists of many small pink to white three-petaled and three-sepaled flowers, ½ inch wide. Found in dry-mesic and dry soils in full sunlight.

IN SEED Plants are 1 to 2 feet tall. Look down for an upright leafless stalk with a round umbel-shaped seed head, with a small capsule at each stem tip exposing four glossy black seeds. The globe-shaped seed head is unique and easily seen in the vegetation. Leaves will be intact at the crown of the plant. Look for a dark green basal tuft of long, narrow flat leaves that taper to a pointed tip. Leaves will appear grass-like, do not have leaf venation, are solid inside, and appear glossy. Crushing a leaf will produce a strong onion odor. Seeds are ¹⁄₁₆ inch (2 mm) long, teardrop-shaped, black, and shiny.

SEED HARVESTING Ripening begins in early October. Each stalk will produce few seeds. Wait until the capsules have opened, exposing the shiny black seeds, before harvesting. Leave light green closed capsules on the stalk to further ripen. Cut the entire head off the stalk when harvesting because seeds shatter easily off the plant; breaking off the head will result in lost seeds. Tumble heads in a large closed container to separate the seeds from the heads. Monitor the plants near ripening time so as not to miss the short harvest window.

0   3

Dodecatheon meadia, shooting star
Primulaceae, primrose family

SEED PRODUCTION ▸ moderate
SEED DURATION ▸ long

0   2

IN FLOWER Flowering begins in mid-May. The inflorescence is an umbel of a few white to pink flowers connected to leafless peduncles. Each flower has five petals that trail behind stamens, forming a point in the front. Found in mesic, dry-mesic, and dry soils in full sunlight and partial shade. This species should be marked with field flags while in flower to ensure it can be found for seed harvesting.

IN SEED Plants are up to 1 foot tall. Look down into woodland openings or in drier areas for a leafless stalk close to the ground with an umbel of branched stems, each tipped with a single brown teardrop-shaped capsule ¼ inch wide by ½ inch long. ▸ Capsules point upward and have a small opening at the top. Leaves will be shriveled and unidentifiable when seed is ripe. Other plants of this species are likely to be growing in the same area. Seeds are ⅟₃₂ inch (1 mm) long, reddish-brown, and nearly round.

SEED HARVESTING Ripening begins in early July. Each stalk produces moderate numbers of seeds. Ripe capsules are dark reddish-brown and remain intact on the stalk full of seeds through the end of summer. Seeds can be harvested either by cutting the capsules off the stalk and carefully holding them upright until they can be placed in a sealed seed-collecting bag or by simply tilting capsules into the bag and pouring the seeds. No further seed cleaning is needed.

Eryngium yuccifolium, rattlesnake master
Apiaceae, parsley family

SEED PRODUCTION ▸ high
SEED DURATION ▸ long

IN FLOWER Flowering begins in mid-July. The inflorescence is a compound umbel consisting of a few egg-shaped flower heads at the terminal end of the stalk. Individual flowers are tiny five-petaled white flowers not easily seen because they are hidden by green florets in the flower head. Sandals made from this plant date back to 8300 BP (Kuttruff, DeHart, and O'Brien 1998). Found in wet-mesic, mesic, and dry-mesic soils in full sunlight.

IN SEED Plants are 2 to 3 feet tall. Look for the compound umbel shape of the seed head, consisting of a round prickly seed head connected to each stem tip. Leaves are linear-shaped, up to 4 inches wide and 12 inches long, taper to a tip, and arranged alternately on the stalk. Opposing spine-like projections along the leaf margins make this species easy to identify in the field. Seeds are ⁵⁄₁₆ inch (8 mm) long, tan, and resemble a prehistoric arthropod in shape.

SEED HARVESTING Ripening begins in early October. Each stalk will produce a high number of seeds. Seeds are ripe when heads turn tan to brown. Seeds are very prickly and hold tightly to the stem into late fall. Wear gloves and cut the stems below the seed head. Harvest only the largest seed heads on each stalk and leave the smaller lateral heads, as they often have few viable seeds. Stomp heads and stems in a utility tub to extract the seeds; then sift the crushed material through ¼-inch-opening hardware screen to separate out the seeds.

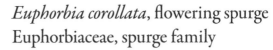

Euphorbia corollata, flowering spurge
Euphorbiaceae, spurge family

SEED PRODUCTION ▸ very few
SEED DURATION ▸ short

IN FLOWER Flowering begins in mid-July and may continue into late August. The inflorescence is umbel-like, consisting of a few small white flowers ¼ inch wide with five petals. This species has separate male and female flowers. Found in mesic, dry-mesic, and dry soils in full sunlight.

IN SEED Plants are 2 to 3 feet tall. Look in dry areas for a lime-green foliated stalk with a branched umbel-like seed head. Each branch can be tipped with a small three-chambered capsule. Each capsule contains three seeds, one seed per chamber. Green leaves are connected to the stalk when seeds are ripe. Leaves are uniform, elongated, and oval, approximately 1 ½ inches long by ½ inch wide, and arranged alternately on the stalk. Latex sap will ooze from a crushed leaf. Seeds are ¹⁄₁₆ inch (2 mm) long, hard and shiny, oval, and vary in color from cream to brown.

0   3

SEED HARVESTING Ripening begins in late August. Each stalk produces very few seeds. Harvesting this species is difficult because of differential seed ripening. It is common to find seeds in all stages of ripening on the same stalk; in fact, ▸ ripe seed capsules can often be found alongside ▸ flowers with immature seeds. Upon ripening, seeds will easily shatter from the capsule with only minimal disturbance. To ensure success in seed collecting, check plants frequently near ripening time and plan to collect seeds multiple times from the same plant. Consider yourself lucky if you can harvest seeds of this species.

Lilium michiganense, Michigan lily
Liliaceae, lily family

SEED PRODUCTION ▸ high
SEED DURATION ▸ medium

IN FLOWER Flowering begins in late June. The inflorescence is a compound umbel of a few large orange flowers up to 3 inches wide, with six spotted, recurved tepals nodding on the flower stalk. Found in wet, wet-mesic, and mesic soils in full sunlight and partial shade.

IN SEED Plants are 3 to 5 feet tall. Look in wet areas for a leafless stalk with a long-stemmed compound umbel, tipped with many large long, oval capsules ¾ inch wide by 1 ½ inches long. All leaves will have fallen off the stalk when seeds are ripe. Michigan lily often grows in wet meadows and in partial shade where adjacent vegetation is shorter, making it easier to spot. A few other solitary plants may grow in close proximity. Seeds are ⁷⁄₁₆ inch (11 mm) long with a dark circular disk center, covered by a tan, triangular membranous layer.

SEED HARVESTING Ripening begins in late September. Each stalk produces high numbers of seeds. Seeds are ripe when capsules are brown. Capsules hold tightly on the stem and should be cut off with scissors. Attempting to pull the capsules off the stalk could result in pulling the lily bulb out of the soil. Split capsules by hand to release the seeds. Each capsule contains about 150 seeds.

Pycnanthemum pilosum, hairy mountain mint
Lamiaceae, mint family

SEED PRODUCTION ▸ high
SEED DURATION ▸ long

0   1

IN FLOWER Flowering begins in late July. The inflorescence is a flat compound umbel of small light green flower heads ¼ inch across, with a few creamy-white tube-shaped, lobed flowers perched on top. Found in mesic and dry-mesic soils in full sunlight and partial shade.

IN SEED Plants are 2 to 3 feet tall. Look for a foliated stalk with a flat compound umbel of brown disk-shaped seed heads about ⅝ inch in diameter. Each seed head consists of densely packed small vertical tubes that contain seeds. Leaves remain attached to the stalk when seeds are initially ripe but completely fall off after a killing frost. Leaves are lance-shaped, sessile, and arranged opposite on the stalk. The stalk is square. All parts of the plant are covered in soft fuzzy hair. Seeds are ⅟₃₂ inch (1 mm) long, oval, and dark brown.

SEED HARVESTING Ripening begins in late September. Each stalk produces high numbers of seeds. The seeds are ripe when the seed heads turn grayish-brown. Seed-head clusters can be broken from stems, but it is faster to cut the entire seed head off the stalk. Harvesting seeds of this species will produce a strong mint odor. Vigorously rub seed heads and stems against ⅛-inch-opening hardware screen placed over a utility tub to separate seeds from heads. Sift the tub material through a standard 20-mesh screen sieve to separate out the seeds. Seed heads remain on the stalk into late fall.

Pycnanthemum tenuifolium, slender mountain mint
Lamiaceae, mint family

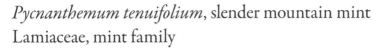

SEED PRODUCTION ▸ high
SEED DURATION ▸ long

IN FLOWER Flowering begins in early July. The inflorescence is a flat compound umbel of small light green
flower heads ⅛ inch across, with a few creamy-white
tube-shaped lobed flowers perched on top. Found in
mesic and dry-mesic soils in full sunlight.

IN SEED Plants are 2 to 3 feet tall. Look for a foliated
stalk with a flat compound umbel of brown disk-
shaped seed heads about ¼ inch in diameter. Each seed
head consists of densely packed small vertical tubes
that contain seeds. Leaves remain attached to the stalk
when seeds are initially ripe but completely fall off after
a killing frost. Leaves are narrow and strap-shaped,
with pointed tips, sessile, and arranged opposite on the
stalk. The stalk is square. Leaves and stalk are nearly
hairless. Seeds are ¹⁄₃₂ inch (1 mm) long, oval, and dark
brown.

SEED HARVESTING Ripening begins in late September.
Each stalk produces high numbers of seeds. Seed heads
will turn grayish-brown when ripe. Seed-head clusters
can be broken from stems when harvesting, but it is
faster to cut the entire seed head off the stalk. Harvesting seeds of this species will produce a strong mint
odor. Vigorously rub seed heads and stems against
⅛-inch-opening hardware screen placed over a utility
tub to separate seeds from heads. Sift the tub material
through a standard 20-mesh screen sieve to separate
out the seeds. Seed heads remain on the stalk into
late fall.

0   1

Pycnanthemum virginianum, common mountain mint, Lamiaceae, mint family

SEED PRODUCTION ▸ high
SEED DURATION ▸ long

IN FLOWER Flowering begins in mid-July. The inflorescence is a flat compound umbel of small light green flower heads ⅛ inch across with a few creamy-white tube-shaped lobed flowers perched on top. Found in wet-mesic and mesic soils in full sunlight.

IN SEED Plants are 2 to 3 feet tall. Look for a foliated stalk with a flat compound umbel of brown disk-shaped seed heads about ¼ inch in diameter. Each seed head consists of densely packed small vertical tubes that contain seeds. Leaves remain attached to the stalk when seeds are initially ripe but fall off after a killing frost. Leaves are lance-shaped, with a pointed tip, sessile, hairless, and arranged opposite on the stalk. The stalk is square and has some hair. Seeds are 1/32 inch (1 mm) long, oval, and dark brown. This species grows in patches of many plants.

SEED HARVESTING Ripening begins in late September. Each stalk produces high numbers of seeds. Seed heads will turn grayish-brown when ripe. Seed-head clusters can be broken from stems when harvesting, but it is faster to cut the entire seed head off the stalk. Harvesting seeds of this species will produce a strong mint odor. Vigorously rub seed heads and stems against ⅛-inch-opening hardware screen placed over a utility tub to separate seeds from heads. Sift the tub material through a standard 20-mesh screen sieve to separate out the seeds. Seed heads remain on the stalk into late fall.

Silphium integrifolium, rosinweed
Asteraceae, daisy family

SEED PRODUCTION ▸ moderate
SEED DURATION ▸ medium

IN FLOWER Flowering begins in mid-July. The inflorescence is an umbel of a few large daisy-shaped flower heads up to 3 inches wide, with yellow rays arranged around a gold disk center. Found in mesic and dry-mesic soils in full sunlight.

IN SEED Plants are 4 to 5 feet tall. Look for a tall upright and foliated stalk with an umbel of large seed heads 1¼ inches wide with large oval bracts surrounding the outer rim of the head. Some leaves may be attached and intact when seeds are ripe. Leaves are wide, oval, with slightly serrate margins and a prominent midvein, sessile, and arranged opposite on the stalk. Seeds are large — ⁷⁄₁₆ inch (11 mm) long — with a plump, dark brown-black oval center surrounded by a tan membrane.

SEED HARVESTING Ripening begins in mid-September. Each stalk produces moderate numbers of seeds. A tan to brown coloration of the seed head indicates that seeds are ripe. Seed heads can be broken off the stems when hand-harvesting. Seeds are located in the head between the bracts and the center disk flower. Don't give up if the flower heads look like parts have fallen off the stalk. ▸ The center disk often drops out of the seed head first, exposing a whorled layer of seeds that can still be harvested. Stomp seed heads in a utility tub to dislodge the seeds from the heads. Sift the crushed material through ⅜-inch-opening hardware screen to separate out the seeds.

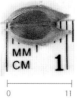

MM
CM 1

0   11

1 *Tradescantia bracteata*, prairie spiderwort
Commelinaceae, spiderwort family

SEED PRODUCTION ▸ few
SEED DURATION ▸ short

IN FLOWER Flowering begins in mid-May. The inflorescence is an umbel of blue to rose-purple three-petaled flowers with blue hair and gold stamens in the center. Found in dry-mesic and dry soils in full sunlight and partial shade. This species should be marked with field flags while in flower to ensure it can be found for seed harvesting.

IN SEED Plants are 1 to 2 feet tall. Look in dry areas for a short green foliated stalk with a reflexed umbel of brown, yellow, and some green seed heads. ▸ Two long bract leaves, similar in shape to basal leaves, extend out from the middle of the seed cluster. Fine fuzzy hair is easily seen. The long linear-shaped leaves have a distinctive fold, taper to a pointed tip, and are arranged alternately on the stalk. A clear gooey sap like cow slobber will ooze from a broken leaf. Seeds are ⅛ inch (3 mm) long, grayish-brown, and oval with pits and ridges.

0   3

SEED HARVESTING Ripening begins in mid-June. This species produces few seeds. Harvesting prairie spiderwort is tricky; it has a long flowering time, and the seeds easily shatter. Do not wait to harvest seeds until the entire seed head is brown, because a lot of seeds will have shattered. Collect when two-thirds of the heads are yellow and brown with a few green heads. Place seed heads on a tarp with a box fan blowing over them. Turn material over three times daily for several days to separate the seeds from the seed heads. Sift material through a standard 10-mesh screen sieve to separate out the seeds.

Tradescantia ohiensis, Ohio spiderwort
Commelinaceae, spiderwort family

SEED PRODUCTION ▸ few
SEED DURATION ▸ short

IN FLOWER Flowering begins in late May. The inflorescence is an umbel of blue to rose-purple three-petaled flowers with blue hair and gold stamens in the center. Found in mesic, dry-mesic, and dry soils in full sunlight and partial shade.

IN SEED Plants are 1 ½ to 2 ½ feet tall. Look in mesic and dry areas for a short green foliated stalk with a reflexed umbel of brown, yellow, and some green seed heads. ▸ Two long bract leaves, similar in shape to basal leaves, extend out from the middle of the seed cluster. Unlike prairie spiderwort, the seed heads are hairless. Leaves are long, linear, and have a distinctive fold. They taper to a pointed tip and are arranged alternately on the stalk. A clear gooey sap like cow slobber will ooze from a broken leaf. Seeds are ⅛ inch (3 mm) long, grayish-brown, and oval with pits and ridges.

SEED HARVESTING Ripening begins in late June. This species produces few seeds. Harvesting Ohio spiderwort is tricky; it has a long flowering time, and seeds easily shatter. Do not wait to harvest seeds until the entire seed head is brown, because a lot of seeds will have shattered. Collect when two-thirds of the heads are yellow and brown with some green heads. To separate the seeds, place the seed heads on a tarp with a box fan blowing over them. Turn material over three times daily for several days to separate the seeds from the seed heads. Sift material through a standard 10-mesh screen sieve to separate out the seeds.

0   3

Veronicastrum virginicum, Culver's root
Scrophulariaceae, figwort family

SEED PRODUCTION ▸ high
SEED DURATION ▸ long

IN FLOWER Flowering begins in mid-July. The inflorescence is an umbel of terminal spikes consisting of small white tube-shaped flowers ⅛ inch wide, with thread-like stamens protruding from the tube. The flowering spikes look like a candelabra on the stalk. Found in wet-mesic, mesic, and dry-mesic soils in full sunlight and partial shade.

IN SEED Plants are 3 to 4 feet tall. Look in areas with wetter soils for a brown or black stalk with an umbel of terminal spikes. Each spike is made up of numerous tiny hard capsules ¹⁄₁₆ inch wide by ⅛ inch long. Some leaves may be attached to the stalk when seeds are ripe. Leaves are elongated, oval, and taper to a pointed tip with serrate margins. Leaves are arranged on the stalk in whorls of four to five leaves. Soon after seed ripening, the entire flowering stalk and leaves turn black, so also look for this color variant in the field. Seeds are dust-like, less than ¹⁄₆₄ inch (0.5 mm) long, tan, and oval.

0   2

SEED HARVESTING Ripening begins in early October. Each stalk produces high numbers of seeds. Brown or black capsules indicate that seeds are ripe. Cut the spike off the stalk below the capsules to harvest the seeds. Stomp capsules and stems vigorously in a utility tub to dislodge the seeds. Sift the tub material through a standard 35-mesh screen sieve to separate out the seeds. Capsules and seeds remain on the stalk into late fall.

Zizia aurea, golden alexanders
Apiaceae, parsley family

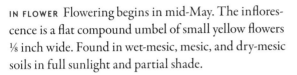

SEED PRODUCTION ▸ few
SEED DURATION ▸ long

IN FLOWER Flowering begins in mid-May. The inflorescence is a flat compound umbel of small yellow flowers ⅛ inch wide. Found in wet-mesic, mesic, and dry-mesic soils in full sunlight and partial shade.

IN SEED Plants are 2 to 3 feet tall. Look inside the grass canopy for a short foliated stalk with a compound umbel tipped with seeds. Some leaves on the upper portion of the stalk are attached and intact when seeds are ripe. Leaves on the upper stalk are compound with three distinct leaflet lobes. Each leaflet is oval with serrate margins and arranged alternately on the stalk. Seeds are 3/16 inch (5 mm) long, oval, and slightly curved. Seeds will vary in color from tan to light brown to dark brown and have linear raised ridges from end to end.

SEED HARVESTING Ripening begins in early September. Each stalk produces few numbers of seeds. Seeds are ripe when they are brown. Cut umbels off the stalk when harvesting. Seeds can be easily separated from any remaining stems by lightly rubbing against ¼-inch-opening hardware screen placed over a utility tub. Seeds can remain on some stalks well into fall if protected from the wind.

Desmanthus illinoensis, Illinois bundleflower
Helenium autumnale, sneezeweed
Helianthus grosseserratus, saw-tooth sunflower
Rudbeckia subtomentosa, fragrant coneflower

Artemisia ludoviciana,
white sage

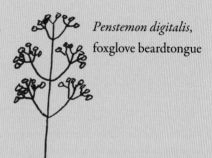

Penstemon digitalis,
foxglove beardtongue

Achillea millefolium, western yarrow
Parthenium integrifolium, wild quinine
Phlox pilosa, prairie phlox

PART SEVEN

Seeds in Panicles without Pappus Bristles

Desmodium canadense, showy tick trefoil

Potentilla arguta, tall cinquefoil

Achillea millefolium, western yarrow
Asteraceae, daisy family

SEED PRODUCTION ▸ moderate
SEED DURATION ▸ long

IN FLOWER Flowering begins in early June. The inflorescence is a terminal flat panicle of corymb clusters of very small, ⅛-inch-wide, white five-petaled flower heads. Found in mesic, dry-mesic, and dry soils in full sunlight.

IN SEED Plants are 2 to 3 feet tall. Look for a terminal seed head retaining the flat panicle shape, light brown in color, and connected to a nearly leafless brown upright stalk. The panicle consists of many individual seed heads ⁵⁄₁₆ inch wide by ¼ inch long, with densely packed, pointed tip bracts that look like miniature pinecones. Any leaves left connected to the stalk will be shriveled and unidentifiable. Sometimes green leaves may occur around the base of the stalk. These will be pinnately compound with leaflets so small that they appear fern-like. Seeds are ¹⁄₁₆ inch (2 mm) long, oval, and tan.

SEED HARVESTING Ripening begins in mid-September. Each stalk will produce moderate numbers of seeds. Seeds are ripe when heads are light brown. It is best to cut the entire head off the stalk when harvesting seeds. Lightly rub flower heads against ⅛-inch-opening wire screen over a utility tub to separate seeds from heads. Sift the tub material with a standard 20-mesh screen sieve to separate out the seeds. Seed heads remain on the stalk into late fall, so check for seeds by crushing a few heads if harvesting late in the season.

Artemisia ludoviciana, white sage
Asteraceae, daisy family

SEED PRODUCTION ▸ high
SEED DURATION ▸ long

0   3

IN FLOWER Flowering begins in late August. The inflorescence is a panicle of numerous flower heads consisting of tiny cream-colored ray flowers, less than ⅛ inch wide, and dark disk flower centers barely visible without magnification. Found in mesic, dry-mesic, and dry soils in full sunlight and partial shade.

IN SEED Plants are 2 to 3 feet tall. Look for a nearly upright multibranched stalk with white foliage. A hand lens will reveal that the white coloration is from twisted, matted hair. Clusters of very small seed heads, also covered in fine white matted hair, are positioned along the upper part of the branched stems. Each seed head is only ⅛ inch wide by ⅛ inch long with a dark center. Crushing any part of this plant produces a strong sage odor. The tiny seeds are 1/32 inch (1 mm) long, narrow, brown, and oval, tapering to a point on one end.

SEED HARVESTING Ripening begins in mid-October. Each stalk can produce high numbers of seeds. It is best to wait until after a killing frost to harvest seeds to ensure for ripeness because seed heads remain white. Cutting the entire seed head off at the main stalk is the most efficient method to harvest this species. Vigorously rub seed heads and stems against ⅛-inch-opening wire screen over a utility tub to separate heads and seeds from stems. Sift this material through a standard 30-mesh screen sieve to separate out the seeds. Seed heads remain on the stalk into winter.

Desmanthus illinoensis, Illinois bundleflower
Fabaceae, legume family

SEED PRODUCTION ▸ high
SEED DURATION ▸ medium

IN FLOWER Flowering begins in mid-July. The inflorescence is a globe-shaped panicle consisting of white flowers and covered with thread-like stamens. Each head connects to a leafless peduncle emanating from the upper leaf axils. Found in dry-mesic and dry soils in full sunlight.

IN SEED Plants are 3 to 4 feet tall. Look in drier soils for a slightly leaning stalk with leaves that appear fern-like, coupled with prominent reddish-brown globe-shaped pod clusters on long leafless stems located in the upper leaf axils. Many green leaves are connected to the stalk when seeds are ripe. Leaves are twice even-pinnately compound. A single leaf has up to 850 very small oval leaflets that make this plant look fern-like from a distance. Look for reddish-brown globe-shaped pod clusters, approximately 1 inch in diameter, on a stalk. Each pod cluster contains forty or more individual pods that are ¼ inch wide by ¾ inch long. Seeds are ⅛ inch (3 mm) long, oval, and brown.

SEED HARVESTING Ripening begins in early September. Each stalk produces high numbers of seeds. Pick only the dark reddish-brown pods and leave the green pods to ripen on the plant. Pods are easy to hand-harvest, but check for seeds. Pod clusters can remain on the stalk into late fall but may not contain any seeds. Vigorously rub pods against ⅛-inch-opening wire screen placed over a utility tub to break apart the pods. Sift the material through a standard 10-mesh screen sieve to separate out the seeds.

Desmodium canadense, showy tick trefoil
Fabaceae, legume family

SEED PRODUCTION ▸ moderate
SEED DURATION ▸ medium

IN FLOWER Flowering begins in mid-July. The inflorescence is a panicle of branched racemes consisting of small pea-shaped pink flowers. Found in wet-mesic, mesic, and dry-mesic soils in full sunlight and partial shade.

IN SEED Plants are 3 to 4 feet tall. Look for one or more leaning stalks with an open panicle consisting of many brown multisegmented pods on the branched stems. Seedpods (loments) consist of three to four segments ¼ inch wide and up to 1 inch long oriented lengthwise perpendicular to the stem. A few lower leaves may remain on the stalk when the seeds are ripe. Compound leaves have three distinctive oval leaflets and are arranged alternately on the stalk. Leaves and stalk are covered with fine fuzzy hair. Pods are covered with tiny hooked hair like Velcro; it is likely this species will locate you first in the field to make an addition to your wardrobe. Seeds are ⅛ inch (3 mm) long, bean-shaped, and tan, light brown, or dark brown.

SEED HARVESTING Ripening begins in late September. Each stalk produces moderate numbers of seeds. This species flowers for long periods, and there may be differential ripening on a single plant. Pods are ripe when they turn from green to brown. Cut the entire panicle off at the main stalk when most of the pods are brown. Vigorously rub pods and stems repeatedly against ⅛-inch-opening wire screen placed over a utility tub to break apart the pods. Sift the material through a standard 10-mesh screen sieve to separate out the seeds.

0   3

Helenium autumnale, sneezeweed
Asteraceae, daisy family

SEED PRODUCTION ▸ high
SEED DURATION ▸ medium

IN FLOWER Flowering begins in early August. The inflorescence is an open panicle of daisy-shaped flower heads of yellow rays with distinctive notches at their tips and a dome-shaped yellowish-brown center. Found in wet and wet-mesic soils in full sunlight and partial shade.

IN SEED Plants are 2 to 4 feet tall. Look in wetter areas for a foliated stalk with an open panicle consisting of many small brown globe-shaped seed heads ½ inch wide. The stalk will have small but visible soft flaps or wings that extend down its entire length. ▸ Wings on the stalk are actually leaf margins. Some green leaves will remain connected when the seeds are ripe. Leaves are elongated, oval, taper to a pointed tip, sessile, and arranged alternately on the stalk. It is likely that many other plants of this species will be found in the same area. Seeds are ¹⁄₁₆ inch (2 mm) long, tan, and oval.

SEED HARVESTING Ripening begins in early October. Each stalk produces high numbers of seeds. A tan to brown flower head will indicate the seeds are ripe. Seed heads are easily removed from the stalk by hand-harvesting and usually break apart into lots of small pieces. Lightly rubbing the harvested material through a standard 20-mesh screen sieve will separate out the seeds. Seed heads can remain mostly intact on the stalk up to a month after ripening.

0   2

Helianthus grosseserratus, saw-tooth sunflower, Asteraceae, daisy family

SEED PRODUCTION ▸ few
SEED DURATION ▸ long

MM

0   4

IN FLOWER Flowering begins in early August. The inflorescence is a panicle of daisy-shaped flower heads with yellow rays and gold disk centers. Found in wet-mesic, mesic, and dry-mesic soils in full sunlight and partial shade.

IN SEED Plants are 5 to 7 feet tall. Look for the tallest foliated stalks in wet areas. Each stalk consists of a panicle of tan, brown, or black dome-shaped seed heads near the upper end. Bracts under the seed head are reflexed. Leaves are large, approximately 1 ½ inches wide and up to 7 inches long, and taper to a point, with serrate margins, and arranged alternately on the stalk. It is common to find many saw-tooth sunflowers in close proximity to one another. Seeds are ⁵⁄₃₂ inch (4 mm) long, lance-shaped, and have a blotchy cream and brown coloration.

SEED HARVESTING Ripening begins in mid-October. Each stalk produces few seeds. Cut seed heads off the main stalk when harvesting. Some flower heads may have few or no seeds at all, so it is wise to crush a head and check for seeds periodically while harvesting. Stomp seed heads and stems in a utility tub to dislodge the seeds. Sift crushed material through a standard 10-mesh screen sieve to separate out the seeds. Seed heads can remain on the stalk into late fall.

Parthenium integrifolium, wild quinine
Asteraceae, daisy family

SEED PRODUCTION ▸ few
SEED DURATION ▸ long

IN FLOWER Flowering begins in mid-June. The inflorescence is a flat terminal panicle of corymb clusters consisting of many small white flower heads, ¼ inch wide, that look like miniature cauliflowers. Found in mesic, dry-mesic, and dry soils in full sunlight.

IN SEED Plants are 2 to 3 feet tall. Look for a foliated stalk with a large, almost black, flat terminal panicle consisting of many smaller seed heads. Leaves are lance-shaped with prominent serrate margins, sessile, and arranged alternately on the stalk. Large ovate basal leaves connect to long petioles at the ground level around the stalk. Leaves have a prominent midvein and feel rough when rubbed. Seeds are ¹⁄₁₆ inch (2 mm) long, black, and teardrop-shaped.

SEED HARVESTING Ripening begins in mid-September. The seed head for wild quinine is quite large and would appear to produce a lot of seeds but in reality produces few seeds. Seed heads are grayish-black when seeds are ripe. Crush a few small heads between your fingers to ensure some seeds are present when harvesting. Cut the entire head off at the main stalk to harvest. Vigorously stomp seed heads in a utility tub to break heads apart and release the seeds. Sift the tub material through ⅛-inch-opening hardware screen to separate out the seeds. This species holds its seed heads into late fall.

Penstemon digitalis, foxglove beardtongue
Scrophulariaceae, figwort family

SEED PRODUCTION ▸ high
SEED DURATION ▸ long

IN FLOWER Flowering begins in mid-June. The inflorescence is a panicle of flower clusters consisting of white to light pink tube-shaped flowers. Each flower has three lower and two upper lobes. Found in mesic and dry-mesic soils in full sunlight and partial shade.

IN SEED Plants are 2 to 3 feet tall. Look for a foliated stalk with a panicle of tan to brown teardrop-shaped hardened capsules, each approximately ¼ inch wide by ⅜ inch long. Capsules are connected at their wide end to branched stem tips with their narrow ends pointing upward. Leaves are lance-shaped with dentate margins, sessile, and arranged opposite on the stalk. Leaves have a prominent midvein and feel smooth when rubbed. Many plants of this species are likely to be growing in the same area. Seeds are ¹⁄₃₂ inch (1 mm) long, tan, and hexagonal with raised ridges on one side.

SEED HARVESTING Ripening begins in early October. Each stalk produces high numbers of seeds. Capsules will turn from green to light brown when ripe. Cut all the capsules off the main stalk when harvesting. Crushing the capsules is necessary to release the seeds. Vigorously stomp the capsules and stems in a utility tub to crush the capsules. Sift the crushed material through a standard 20-mesh screen sieve to separate out the seeds. Be prepared for a pungent odor of sweaty socks when cleaning seeds of this species. Capsules remain closed and retain their seeds into late fall.

0   3

Phlox pilosa, prairie phlox
Polemoniaceae, phlox family

SEED PRODUCTION ▸ very few
SEED DURATION ▸ short

IN FLOWER Flowering begins in mid-May. The inflorescence is a compact terminal panicle consisting of five-lobed funnel-shaped flowers. Colors vary from shades of white, red, lavender, and pink. Found in mesic, dry-mesic, and dry soils in full sunlight and partial shade. This species should be marked with field flags while in flower to ensure it can be found for seed harvesting.

IN SEED Plants are 1 to 2 feet tall. Look in drier areas for short, foliated, delicate tan stalks with a compact terminal cluster of small tan capsules. ▸ Capsules are oval and very small, only ⅛ inch wide by ⅛ inch long. At the base of each capsule are five narrow pointed sepals. Upon ripening, the sepals pull away from and expose the capsule. Leaves are very narrow and hairy, lance-shaped, sessile, and arranged opposite on the stalk. It is likely that other plants of this species will be found in the same area. Seeds are ¹⁄₁₆ inch (2 mm) long, black, oval, and covered with very small dimples.

SEED HARVESTING Ripening begins in late June. Each stalk produces very few seeds. Exposed tan capsules indicate the seeds are ripe. Cut all the capsules off the main stalk when harvesting. This species ejects its seeds off the plant upon ripening, so check plants every few days. Place harvested seeds and stalks in a breathable, sealed cloth bag to dry, and the seeds will eject from the head in a few days.

0   3

Potentilla arguta, tall cinquefoil
Rosaceae, rose family

SEED PRODUCTION ▸ high
SEED DURATION ▸ long

0   2

IN FLOWER Flowering begins in late July. The inflorescence is a compact terminal panicle of creamy-white five-petaled flowers with gold centers. Found in dry-mesic and dry soils in full sunlight.

IN SEED Plants are 2 to 3 feet tall. Look in drier areas for a knee-high foliated stalk with a compact terminal panicle that appears club-like. The panicle consists of clusters of reddish-brown soft-bodied capsules. Capsules are teardrop-shaped, ⅜ inch wide by ⅜ inch long, with the widest part connected to short stems and the narrow ends pointing upward. Leaves are odd-pinnately compound, with double-serrate leaflet margins, and arranged alternately on the stalk. Stalk and leaves are covered with fine soft hair. Other plants of this species will be found in the same area. Seeds are ¹⁄₃₂ inch (1 mm) long, balloon-shaped, smooth, and tan.

SEED HARVESTING Ripening begins in late September. Each stalk produces high numbers of seeds. Capsules turn reddish-brown when ripe. Cut the entire capsule cluster off the main stalk when harvesting. The capsule is soft and filled with loose seeds, so seed extraction is quite easy. Lightly rub pods against a standard 30-mesh screen sieve to separate seeds from nonseed capsule particles. Capsules remain mostly closed and retain seeds into late fall.

Rudbeckia subtomentosa, fragrant coneflower
Asteraceae, daisy family

SEED PRODUCTION ▸ high
SEED DURATION ▸ long

IN FLOWER Flowering begins in early August. The inflorescence is a flat terminal panicle of a few large single-stemmed daisy-shaped flower heads up to 3 inches wide, with yellow rays and a reddish-brown dome-shaped center. Found in wet-mesic, mesic, dry-mesic, and dry soils in full sunlight and partial shade.

IN SEED Plants are 3 to 5 feet tall. Look for an upright green foliated stalk with a flat terminal panicle consisting a few large brown dome-shaped seed heads connected to branched stem tips. ▸ Short narrow and pointed tan bracts radiate from under the dome. Leaf shape varies according to its location on the stalk. Upper leaves are ovate, with serrate margins and pointed tips, and arranged alternately on the stalk. Lower leaves have three distinct lobes. Each lobe is elongated and oval, tapering to a pointed tip, with serrate margins. Seeds are ⅛ inch (3 mm) long, black, and banana-shaped.

SEED HARVESTING Ripening begins in late September. Each stalk produces high numbers of seeds. The seeds are ripe when seed heads turn brown. Cut seed heads off the stalk when harvesting. Seed heads remain on the stalks well into fall but may have shattered seeds. Periodically crush the seed head in your palm to check for seeds if harvesting later in the season. Vigorously rub seed heads and stems against ⅛-inch-opening hardware screen placed over a utility tub to separate the seeds from the heads. Sift the material through a standard 14-mesh screen sieve to separate out the seeds.

Brickellia eupatorioides, false boneset
Eupatorium altissimum, tall boneset
Solidago speciosa, showy goldenrod

Vernonia fasciculata,
ironweed

Eupatorium perfoliatum,
boneset

Solidago nemoralis, field goldenrod

PART EIGHT

Seeds in Panicles with Pappus Bristles

Symphyotrichum ericoides, heath aster

Symphyotrichum laeve, smooth blue aster
Symphyotrichum novae-angliae, New England aster

Euthamia graminifolia, grass-leaved goldenrod
Oligoneuron rigidum, stiff goldenrod

Brickellia eupatorioides, false boneset
Asteraceae, daisy family

SEED PRODUCTION ▸ high
SEED DURATION ▸ short

IN FLOWER Flowering begins in mid-August. The inflorescence is a panicle of corymb clusters of small creamy-white thread-like disk flowers ⅜ inch wide. Found in mesic, dry-mesic, and dry soils in full sunlight.

IN SEED Plants are 2 to 4 feet tall. Look in dry areas within the prairie vegetation for a foliated upright stalk with an open panicle of dense clusters of brilliant white dome-shaped pappus bristles. The white bristles will stand out in contrast to the fall colors of other plants. Leaves are connected and still green to yellow when the seeds are ripe. ▸ Leaves are elongated and oval, taper to a point at the tip, and have unevenly spaced and sized serrated teeth on the leaf margins. They will be arranged alternately on the stalk and have a single mid-vein on the surface. It is likely that other plants will be present. Seeds are ⁵⁄₃₂ inch (4 mm) long, gray, and rod-shaped, with a white pappus bristle tuft on the end.

SEED HARVESTING Ripening begins in mid-September. Each stalk can produce high numbers of seeds. White dome-shaped pappus bristles indicate the seeds are ripe. It is best to cut the entire panicle off the stalk when harvesting. Rub seed heads and stems against ¼-inch-opening wire screen placed over a utility tub to separate out the seeds. Try to harvest seeds close to the ripening time because they easily shatter in the wind.

Eupatorium altissimum, tall boneset
Asteraceae, daisy family

SEED PRODUCTION ▸ high
SEED DURATION ▸ medium

0   5

IN FLOWER Flowering begins in early August. The inflorescence is a large terminal panicle of small white flower heads ⅛ inch wide. Found in mesic and dry-mesic soils in full sunlight and partial shade.

IN SEED Plants are 3 to 5 feet tall. Look in drier areas for tall foliated stalks above the grass canopy and for a large terminal panicle of dense white pappus bristles. Green leaves may be connected to the stalk when seeds are ripe. Leaves are elongated, oval, ½ inch wide and up to 5 inches long, tapering at each end, and arranged alternately on the stalk. ▸ Leaves have three distinct parallel veins with serrate margins on the upper half. Hair is present on the stalk. It is likely that other plants of this species will be present in the same area. Seeds are ⅛ inch (3 mm) long, brown, and rod-shaped, tapering at one end with a tuft of white pappus bristles connected to the other end.

SEED HARVESTING Ripening begins in late September. Each stalk produces high numbers of seeds. Cut the entire seed head off at the main stalk to harvest the seeds. Lightly rub seed heads and stems against ¼-inch-opening hardware screen over a utility tub to separate out the seeds. Try to harvest seeds close to the ripening time because they easily shatter in the wind.

Eupatorium perfoliatum, boneset
Asteraceae, daisy family

SEED PRODUCTION ▸ high
SEED DURATION ▸ medium

IN FLOWER Flowering begins in mid-August. The inflorescence is a large terminal panicle of corymb clusters of small white flower heads ⅛ inch wide. Found in wet and wet-mesic soils in full sunlight and partial shade.

IN SEED Plants are 2 to 3 feet tall. Look in the very wettest areas for a green foliated stalk with a large terminal whitish-tan panicle. The panicle consists of dense clusters of whitish-tan pappus bristles on numerous small seed heads. Leaves are ovate, up to 5 inches long, with serrate margins, and taper to a pointed tip. ▸ Leaves are sessile and fused with the opposing leaf on the stalk. Venation on leaves appears puckered, and hair will be prominently visible. Seeds are ¹⁄₁₆ inch (2 mm) long, banana-shaped, and dark gray, with a short tuft of white pappus bristles connected to one end.

SEED HARVESTING Ripening begins in early October. Each stalk produces high numbers of seeds. Seeds are ripe when pappus bristles open to form a white dome shape on each seed head. Cut the entire seed head off at the main stalk to harvest seeds. Vigorously rub seed heads and stems against ¼-inch-opening hardware screen placed over a utility tub to separate out the seeds. Seeds easily shatter off the stalk after ripening, so harvest near ripening time to maximize collection.

0   3

Euthamia graminifolia, grass-leaved goldenrod, Asteraceae, daisy family

SEED PRODUCTION ▸ high
SEED DURATION ▸ medium

IN FLOWER Flowering begins in mid-August. The inflorescence is a flat terminal panicle of numerous small yellow flower heads ⅛ inch wide. Found in wet-mesic, mesic, and dry-mesic soils in full sunlight and partial shade.

IN SEED Plants are 2 to 3 feet tall. Look in wet areas for a green foliated stalk with a flat terminal whitish-tan panicle. The panicle consists of dense clusters of whitish-tan pappus bristles on numerous small seed heads. This species produces extensive rhizomes and can be abundant in wetter soils. In addition, each plant typically produces multiple stalks. Leaves are narrow and strap-like, approximately ¼ inch wide and up to 3 inches long, have a prominent midvein, are sessile, and arranged alternately on the stalk. Seeds are ¹⁄₃₂ inch (1 mm) long, oval, tan, with a small pappus bristle tuft connected to one end.

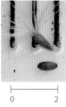

0   2

SEED HARVESTING Ripening begins in early October. Each stalk produces high numbers of seeds. Seeds are ripe when pappus bristles open to form a white dome shape on each seed head. Cut the entire seed head off at the main stalk to harvest seeds. Vigorously rub seed heads and stems against ⅛-inch-opening hardware screen placed over a utility tub to separate out and extract the seeds.

Oligoneuron rigidum, stiff goldenrod
Asteraceae, daisy family

SEED PRODUCTION ▸ high
SEED DURATION ▸ long

IN FLOWER Flowering begins in early September. The inflorescence is a terminal panicle of corymb clusters of small bright yellow ray-and-disk flower heads ⅜ inch wide. Found in wet-mesic, mesic, and dry-mesic soils in full sunlight and partial shade.

IN SEED Plants are 3 to 4 feet tall. Look in well-drained drier areas for a foliated stalk with a terminal panicle consisting of densely packed bright white pappus bristles. Leaves are ovate, with notched (crenate) margins, sessile, and arranged alternately on the stalk. Elongated oval basal leaves connected to long petioles may be found on the ground around the stalk base. Many plants are likely to be growing in the same area. Seeds are approximately ⅛ inch (3 mm) long, banana-shaped, and white with dark lines running down the length.

SEED HARVESTING Ripening begins in early October. Each stalk produces high numbers of seeds. White fluffed-out, dome-shaped pappus bristle tufts indicate the seeds are ripe. Seed heads hold tightly and need to be cut from the stalk when harvesting. The seed heads on this species are very large, so bring a big bag when harvesting. Vigorously rub the seed heads against ¼-inch-opening hardware screen over a utility tub to separate out the seeds. Wear gloves when screening since the woody seed heads are hard on bare skin.

0   4

Solidago nemoralis, field goldenrod
Asteraceae, daisy family

SEED PRODUCTION ▸ high
SEED DURATION ▸ medium

0   4

IN FLOWER Flowering begins in mid-August. The inflorescence is a narrow panicle of numerous small yellow flowers ⅛ inch wide. Found in dry-mesic and dry soils in full sunlight and in partial shade.

IN SEED Plants are 1 to 2 feet tall. Look in drier areas for a short, heavily leaning foliated stalk with a narrow panicle of white pappus bristles densely packed around the stalk. Dormant leaves are attached to the stalk when seeds are ripe. Leaves are oblanceolate with slight serrate margins on the upper third, sessile, and arranged alternately on the stalk. Leaves have a prominent midvein and greatly increase in size down the stalk. It is likely that other plants will be growing in the same area. Seeds are ⅟₃₂ inch (1 mm) long, oval, tapering at one end, and dark gray with a short tuft of white pappus bristles connected to the wide end.

SEED HARVESTING Ripening begins in early October. Each stalk produces high numbers of seeds. White fluffed-out pappus bristles indicate that seeds are ripe. Seeds hold tightly, and a hard pull on the stalk when harvesting could uproot the plant's shallow rhizomes from the soil. It is best to cut the seed head off the stalk to harvest. Vigorously rub seed heads and stems against ⅛-inch-opening hardware screen placed over a utility tub to separate out the seeds.

Solidago speciosa, showy goldenrod
Asteraceae, daisy family

SEED PRODUCTION ▸ high
SEED DURATION ▸ medium

IN FLOWER Flowering begins in mid-August. The inflorescence is an erect cone-shaped panicle of densely clustered small yellow flowers ¼ inch wide. Found in mesic, dry-mesic, and dry soils in full sunlight and partial shade.

IN SEED Plants are 3 to 4 feet tall. Look in drier areas for a few closely grouped foliated stalks with a cone-shaped panicle densely packed with bright white pappus bristles. ▸ Stalks have a deep red color that is easily seen in the field. Brown shriveled leaves are attached to the stalk when seeds are ripe. Leaves are oblanceolate with entire margins, sessile, and arranged alternately on the stalk. Leaves increase in size on the stalk from the top to the bottom and feature a prominent midvein. Seeds are 1⁄16 inch (2 mm) long, cream-colored, and rod-shaped, tapering to a point with a short tuft of white pappus bristles connected to the wide end.

SEED HARVESTING Ripening begins in early October. Each stalk produces high numbers of seeds. Seeds are ripe when pappus bristles fluff out and turn white. Cut the entire panicle off the stalk to harvest the seeds. Vigorously rub the seed heads and stems against 1⁄8-inch-opening hardware screen over a utility tub to separate out the seeds. Seeds will remain on the stalk for a few weeks after ripening but will completely shatter off the plant after that.

0   3

Symphyotrichum ericoides, heath aster
Asteraceae, daisy family

SEED PRODUCTION ▸ high
SEED DURATION ▸ long

IN FLOWER Flowering begins in mid-August. The inflorescence is a widely branched panicle of white daisy-shaped flower heads ½ inch wide. Each flower has white rays arranged around a yellow disk center. Found in mesic, dry-mesic, and dry soils in full sunlight and partial shade.

IN SEED Plants are 1 to 3 feet tall. Look in drier areas for a foliated, widely branched main stalk covered with small white and tan dome-shaped pappus bristles. Plant size will vary for this species. Brown shriveled leaves remain attached to the stalk when seeds are ripe. Leaf shape varies somewhat on the stalk, but most are linear-shaped and taper to a pointed tip, sessile, and arranged alternately on the stem. Seeds are 1/32 inch (1 mm) long, dark, and oval, tapering to a point with a small tuft of white pappus bristles connected to the wide end.

0   2

SEED HARVESTING Ripening begins in mid-October. Each stalk produces high numbers of seeds. Seeds are ripe when pappus bristles turn white and fluffy. Cut branched stems bearing seeds off the plant when harvesting. Because of its late seed-ripening time, heath aster may be one of the last species collected in any given year. Vigorously rub seed heads and stems against ⅛-inch-opening hardware screen over a utility tub to separate out the seeds. Seeds remain on the plant into late fall.

Symphyotrichum laeve, smooth blue aster
Asteraceae, daisy family

SEED PRODUCTION ▸ high
SEED DURATION ▸ medium

IN FLOWER Flowering begins in mid-August. The inflorescence is a panicle of daisy-shaped flower heads, 1 inch wide, with blue rays and gold disk centers. Found in mesic and dry-mesic soils in full sunlight and partial shade.

IN SEED Plants are 1 ½ to 2 ½ feet tall. Look in dry areas within the prairie vegetation for an upright foliated stalk about knee high, with a small panicle consisting of cream-colored dome-shaped tufts of pappus bristles approximately ½ inch wide. Brown leaves remain intact on the stalk when seeds are ripe. Leaves are elongated, oval, with entire margins, clasp to the stalk, and are arranged alternately on the stem. Leaves increase in size from the top to the bottom of the stalk. Seeds are ¹⁄₁₆ inch (2 mm) long, brown, and oval, tapering to a point. Each seed will display distinctive linear ribs down its length and is connected to a tuft of cream-colored pappus bristles on one end.

SEED HARVESTING Ripening begins in mid-October. Each stalk produces high numbers of seeds. Seeds are ripe when pappus bristles become dome-shaped and cream-colored. Seeds are easily peeled off the stalk by hand. Lightly rub the seed heads against ⅛-inch-opening hardware screen over a utility tub to separate out the seeds.

Symphyotrichum novae-angliae,
New England aster, Asteraceae, daisy family

SEED PRODUCTION ▸ high
SEED DURATION ▸ long

0   4

IN FLOWER Flowering begins in early September. The inflorescence is a panicle consisting of corymb clusters of daisy-shaped flower heads, 1 inch wide, with purple rays and gold disk centers. Found in wet-mesic, mesic, and dry-mesic soils in full sunlight and partial shade.

IN SEED Plants are 2 to 4 feet tall. Look for a tall foliated stalk with a panicle of tan globe-shaped pappus bristles about ½ inch across. Each globe-shaped seed head is connected to a short stem tip and is easily seen in the field. Leaves remain attached and intact on the stalk when seeds are ripe. Leaves are elongated, oval, with entire margins, ▸ clasp the stalk, and are arranged alternately. The stalk is covered with soft fuzzy hair. Seeds are ¹⁄₁₆ inch (2 mm) long, dark, hairy, oval, and taper to a point. A tuft of tan pappus bristles connects at one end.

SEED HARVESTING Ripening begins in mid-October. Each stalk produces high numbers of seeds. Tan globe-shaped pappus bristles indicate ripe seeds. Seeds can be easily pulled off by hand, but it is more efficient to cut stems off below clusters of seed heads. Lightly rub the seed heads and stems against ¼-inch-opening hardware screen over a utility tub to separate out the seeds. Seeds remain on the stalk for a few weeks after ripening but will completely shatter off the plant after that.

Vernonia fasciculata, ironweed
Asteraceae, daisy family

SEED PRODUCTION ▸ high
SEED DURATION ▸ long

IN FLOWER Flowering begins in early August. The inflorescence is a large terminal panicle of corymb clusters of purple flowers, ⅜ inch wide. Found in wet-mesic and mesic soils in full sunlight and partial shade.

IN SEED Plants are 3 to 5 feet tall. Look in wetter soils for a tall green foliated stalk with a large terminal panicle with a tan to light brown plume of pappus bristles. Leaves are narrow, oval, with serrate margins, and taper to a pointed tip. Leaves have a prominent midvein and are arranged opposite on the stalk. It is likely that many stalks of this species will be found in a group. Seeds are 5⁄32 inch (4 mm) long, oval, and slightly curved with a tuft of tan bristles connected to one end. Seeds will have linear raised ridges from end to end.

SEED HARVESTING Ripening begins in late September. Each stalk produces high numbers of seeds. The pappus bristles turn tan or brown when ripe. Bristles do not fully extend and stay compacted when seeds are ripe, unlike most asters, which fuzz out. Cut the entire seed head off the stalk when harvesting seeds. Vigorously rub the seed heads and stems against ¼-inch-opening hardware screen over a utility tub to separate out the seeds. This species holds its seed heads into late fall.

0   7

Leaf Identification

Leaf Arrangements

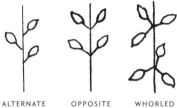

ALTERNATE   OPPOSITE   WHORLED

Adapted from Harris and Harris (2004).

Leaf Connections

PETIOLE   SESSILE   FUSED   CLASPING

Leaf Divisions

SIMPLE   COMPOUND   EVEN-PINNATELY COMPOUND   ODD-PINNATELY COMPOUND   TWICE-DIVIDED COMPOUND

Adapted from Harris and Harris (2004).

Leaf Shapes

LANCEOLATE/LANCE   ELLIPTIC   LINEAR

OBLANCEOLATE   OVAL   OVATE

Adapted from Harris and Harris (2004).

Leaf Margins

ENTIRE   CRENATE   SERRATE   DOUBLE-SERRATE

IRREGULAR SERRATE   DENTATE    LOBED    DISSECTED

Adapted from Harris and Harris (2004).

TABLE 1. Initial flowering (F) and ripening (R) times

Scientific name	Common name	MAY			JUNE			JULY			AUG			SEPT			OCT	
		early	mid	late	early	mid	late	early	mid	late	early	mid	late	early	mid	late	early	mid
Geum triflorum	prairie smoke	F																
Tradescantia bracteata	prairie spiderwort		F			R												
Viola pedatifida	prairie violet	F				R												
Phlox pilosa	prairie phlox		F				R											
Tradescantia ohiensis	Ohio spiderwort			F			R											
Allium canadense	wild garlic				F			R										
Dodecatheon meadia	shooting star		F					R										
Delphinium virescens	prairie larkspur					F			R									
Anemone canadensis	Canada anemone			F						R								
Lithospermum caroliniense	hairy puccoon				F					R								
Anemone cylindrica	thimbleweed						F				R							
Chamaecrista fasciculata	partridge pea							F			R							
Penstemon grandiflorus	large-flowered beardtongue				F							R						
Ceanothus americanus	New Jersey tea						F						R					
Euphorbia corollata	flowering spurge								F				R					
Asclepias tuberosa	butterfly milkweed						F							R				
Desmanthus illinoensis	Illinois bundleflower								F					R				
Onosmodium molle	false gromwell					F								R				
Zizia aurea	golden alexanders													R				
Achillea millefolium	western yarrow		F												R			
Amorpha canescens	leadplant						F								R			

Note: Species are organized by ripening times.

Table continued on following page

TABLE 1. Initial flowering (F) and ripening (R) times

Scientific name	Common name	MAY			JUNE			JULY			AUG			SEPT			OCT	
		early	mid	late	early	mid	late	early	mid	late	early	mid	late	early	mid	late	early	mid
Astragalus canadensis	milk vetch								F						R			
Baptisia bracteata	cream false indigo		F												R			
Brickellia eupatorioides	false boneset											F			R			
Coreopsis palmata	prairie coreopsis					F									R			
Parthenium integrifolium	wild quinine					F									R			
Ratibida pinnata	gray-headed coneflower								F						R			
Silphium integrifolium	rosinweed								F						R			
Silphium laciniatum	compass plant							F							R			
Teucrium canadense	germander							F							R			
Asclepias incarnata	swamp milkweed							F								R		
Asclepias verticillata	whorled milkweed							F								R		
Baptisia alba	white wild indigo				F											R		
Dalea candida	white prairie clover							F								R		
Dalea purpurea	purple prairie clover							F								R		
Desmodium canadense	showy tick trefoil								F							R		
Echinacea pallida	pale purple coneflower					F										R		
Eupatorium altissimum	tall boneset										F					R		
Helianthus pauciflorus	prairie sunflower										F					R		
Heliopsis helianthoides	ox-eye sunflower					F										R		
Lespedeza capitata	round-headed bush clover											F				R		
Liatris pycnostachya	prairie blazing star									F						R		
Lilium michiganense	Michigan lily						F									R		

Note: Species are organized by ripening times.

Table continued on following page

TABLE 1. Initial flowering (F) and ripening (R) times

Scientific name	Common name	MAY			JUNE			JULY			AUG			SEPT			OCT	
		early	mid	late	early	mid	late	early	mid	late	early	mid	late	early	mid	late	early	mid
Monarda fistulosa	wild bergamot								F							R	R	
Monarda punctata	spotted horsemint								F							R	R	
Potentilla arguta	tall cinquefoil									F						R	R	
Pycnanthemum pilosum	hairy mountain mint									F						R	R	
Pycnanthemum tenuifolium	slender mountain mint							F								R	R	
Pycnanthemum virginianum	common mountain mint								F							R	R	
Rudbeckia hirta	black-eyed Susan							F								R	R	
Rudbeckia subtomentosa	fragrant coneflower										F					R	R	
Verbena hastata	blue vervain							F								R	R	
Verbena stricta	hoary vervain						F									R	R	
Vernonia fasciculata	ironweed										F					R	R	
Veronicastrum virginicum	Culver's root								F									R
Allium stellatum	wild prairie onion										F							R
Eryngium yuccifolium	rattlesnake master								F									R
Eupatorium perfoliatum	boneset											F						R
Euthamia graminifolia	grass-leaved goldenrod											F						R
Helenium autumnale	sneezeweed										F							R
Liatris aspera	rough blazing star												F					R
Lobelia siphilitica	great blue lobelia											F						R
Oligoneuron rigidum	stiff goldenrod													F				R
Penstemon digitalis	foxglove beardtongue					F												R
Ruellia humilis	wild petunia								F									R

Table continued on following page

Note: Species are organized by ripening times.

TABLE 1. Initial flowering (F) and ripening (R) times

Scientific name	Common name	MAY			JUNE			JULY			AUG			SEPT			OCT	
		early	mid	late	early	mid	late	early	mid	late	early	mid	late	early	mid	late	early	mid
Solidago nemoralis	field goldenrod											F					R	
Solidago speciosa	showy goldenrod											F					R	
Artemisia ludoviciana	white sage												F					R
Gentiana andrewsii	bottle gentian													F				R
Helianthus grosseserratus	saw-tooth sunflower										F							R
Symphyotrichum ericoides	heath aster											F						R
Symphyotrichum laeve	smooth blue aster											F						R
Symphyotrichum novae-angliae	New England aster													F				R

Note: Species are organized by ripening times.

TABLE 2. Initial ripening time and seed duration after ripening

Scientific name	Common name	Initial ripening time	Very short	Short	Medium	Long
			Duration of seeds on stalk			
Achillea millefolium	western yarrow	mid-September				•
Allium canadense	wild garlic	early July		•		
Allium stellatum	wild prairie onion	early October		•		
Amorpha canescens	leadplant	mid-September				•
Anemone canadensis	Canada anemone	late July		•		
Anemone cylindrica	thimbleweed	early August			•	
Artemisia ludoviciana	white sage	mid-October				•
Asclepias incarnata	swamp milkweed	late September		•		
Asclepias tuberosa	butterfly milkweed	early September		•		
Asclepias verticillata	whorled milkweed	late September		•		
Astragalus canadensis	milk vetch	mid-September				•
Baptisia alba	white wild indigo	late September				•
Baptisia bracteata	cream false indigo	mid-September				•
Brickellia eupatorioides	false boneset	mid-September		•		
Ceanothus americanus	New Jersey tea	late August			•	
Chamaecrista fasciculata	partridge pea	early August			•	
Coreopsis palmata	prairie coreopsis	mid-September				•
Dalea candida	white prairie clover	late September				•
Dalea purpurea	purple prairie clover	late September				•
Delphinium virescens	prairie larkspur	mid-July		•		
Desmanthus illinoensis	Illinois bundleflower	early September			•	
Desmodium canadense	showy tick trefoil	late September			•	
Dodecatheon meadia	shooting star	early July				•
Echinacea pallida	pale purple coneflower	late September				•
Eryngium yuccifolium	rattlesnake master	early October				•
Eupatorium altissimum	tall boneset	late September			•	
Eupatorium perfoliatum	boneset	early October			•	
Euphorbia corollata	flowering spurge	late August		•		
Euthamia graminifolia	grass-leaved goldenrod	early October			•	
Gentiana andrewsii	bottle gentian	mid-October				•
Geum triflorum	prairie smoke	mid-June		•		
Helenium autumnale	sneezeweed	early October			•	
Helianthus grosseserratus	saw-tooth sunflower	mid-October				•
Helianthus pauciflorus	prairie sunflower	late September				•
Heliopsis helianthoides	ox-eye sunflower	late September				•
Lespedeza capitata	round-headed bush clover	late September				•
Liatris aspera	rough blazing star	early October				•
Liatris pycnostachya	prairie blazing star	late September			•	

Note: Very short = a few days or less; short = 2 weeks or less; medium = up to 4 weeks; long = 4 weeks or more.

Table continued on following page

TABLE 2. Initial ripening time and seed duration after ripening

Scientific name	Common name	Initial ripening time	Duration of seeds on stalk			
			Very short	Short	Medium	Long
Lilium michiganense	Michigan lily	late September			•	
Lithospermum caroliniense	hairy puccoon	late July		•		
Lobelia siphilitica	great blue lobelia	early October				•
Monarda fistulosa	wild bergamot	late September				•
Monarda punctata	spotted horsemint	late September				•
Oligoneuron rigidum	stiff goldenrod	early October				•
Onosmodium molle	false gromwell	early September		•		
Parthenium integrifolium	wild quinine	mid-September				•
Penstemon digitalis	foxglove beardtongue	early October				•
Penstemon grandiflorus	large-flowered beardtongue	mid-August				•
Phlox pilosa	prairie phlox	late June		•		
Potentilla arguta	tall cinquefoil	late September				•
Pycnanthemum pilosum	hairy mountain mint	late September				•
Pycnanthemum tenuifolium	slender mountain mint	late September				•
Pycnanthemum virginianum	common mountain mint	late September				•
Ratibida pinnata	gray-headed coneflower	mid-September				•
Rudbeckia hirta	black-eyed Susan	late September				•
Rudbeckia subtomentosa	fragrant coneflower	late September				•
Ruellia humilis	wild petunia	early October				•
Silphium integrifolium	rosinweed	mid-September			•	
Silphium laciniatum	compass plant	mid-September				•
Solidago nemoralis	field goldenrod	early October			•	
Solidago speciosa	showy goldenrod	early October			•	
Symphyotrichum ericoides	heath aster	mid-October				•
Symphyotrichum laeve	smooth blue aster	mid-October			•	
Symphyotrichum novae-angliae	New England aster	mid-October				•
Teucrium canadense	germander	mid-September				•
Tradescantia bracteata	prairie spiderwort	mid-June		•		
Tradescantia ohiensis	Ohio spiderwort	late June		•		
Verbena hastata	blue vervain	late September				•
Verbena stricta	hoary vervain	late September				•
Vernonia fasciculata	ironweed	late September				•
Veronicastrum virginicum	Culver's root	early October				•
Viola pedatifida	prairie violet	mid-June	•			
Zizia aurea	golden alexanders	early September				•

Note: Very short = a few days or less; short = 2 weeks or less; medium = up to 4 weeks; long = 4 weeks or more.

TABLE 3. Number of seeds produced per stalk

Scientific name	Common name	Very few	Few	Moderate	High
Achillea millefolium	western yarrow			•	
Allium canadense	wild garlic	•			
Allium stellatum	wild prairie onion		•		
Amorpha canescens	leadplant			•	
Anemone canadensis	Canada anemone	•			
Anemone cylindrica	thimbleweed			•	
Artemisia ludoviciana	white sage				•
Asclepias incarnata	swamp milkweed			•	
Asclepias tuberosa	butterfly milkweed			•	
Asclepias verticillata	whorled milkweed			•	
Astragalus canadensis	milk vetch			•	
Baptisia alba	white wild indigo				•
Baptisia bracteata	cream false indigo				•
Brickellia eupatorioides	false boneset				•
Ceanothus americanus	New Jersey tea		•		
Chamaecrista fasciculata	partridge pea			•	
Coreopsis palmata	prairie coreopsis		•		
Dalea candida	white prairie clover			•	
Dalea purpurea	purple prairie clover			•	
Delphinium virescens	prairie larkspur		•		
Desmanthus illinoensis	Illinois bundleflower				•
Desmodium canadense	showy tick trefoil			•	
Dodecatheon meadia	shooting star			•	
Echinacea pallida	pale purple coneflower			•	
Eryngium yuccifolium	rattlesnake master				•
Eupatorium altissimum	tall boneset				•
Eupatorium perfoliatum	boneset				•
Euphorbia corollata	flowering spurge	•			
Euthamia graminifolia	grass-leaved goldenrod				•
Gentiana andrewsii	bottle gentian				•
Geum triflorum	prairie smoke	•			
Helenium autumnale	sneezeweed				•
Helianthus grosseserratus	saw-tooth sunflower		•		
Helianthus pauciflorus	prairie sunflower	•			
Heliopsis helianthoides	ox-eye sunflower			•	
Lespedeza capitata	round-headed bush clover		•		
Liatris aspera	rough blazing star				•
Liatris pycnostachya	prairie blazing star				•
Lilium michiganense	Michigan lily				•
Lithospermum caroliniense	hairy puccoon	•			
Lobelia siphilitica	great blue lobelia				•

Note: Very few = fewer than 50; few = 51–200; moderate = 201–500; high = more than 500.

Table continued on following page

TABLE 3. Number of seeds produced per stalk

Scientific name	Common name	Seeds produced per stalk			
		Very few	Few	Moderate	High
Monarda fistulosa	wild bergamot				•
Monarda punctata	spotted horsemint				•
Oligoneuron rigidum	stiff goldenrod				•
Onosmodium molle	false gromwell	•			
Parthenium integrifolium	wild quinine		•		
Penstemon digitalis	foxglove beardtongue				•
Penstemon grandiflorus	large-flowered beardtongue				•
Phlox pilosa	prairie phlox	•			
Potentilla arguta	tall cinquefoil				•
Pycnanthemum pilosum	hairy mountain mint				•
Pycnanthemum tenuifolium	slender mountain mint				•
Pycnanthemum virginianum	common mountain mint				•
Ratibida pinnata	gray-headed coneflower				•
Rudbeckia hirta	black-eyed Susan				•
Rudbeckia subtomentosa	fragrant coneflower				•
Ruellia humilis	wild petunia		•		
Silphium integrifolium	rosinweed			•	
Silphium laciniatum	compass plant			•	
Solidago nemoralis	field goldenrod				•
Solidago speciosa	showy goldenrod				•
Symphyotrichum ericoides	heath aster				•
Symphyotrichum laeve	smooth blue aster				•
Symphyotrichum novae-angliae	New England aster				•
Teucrium canadense	germander		•		
Tradescantia bracteata	prairie spiderwort		•		
Tradescantia ohiensis	Ohio spiderwort		•		
Verbena hastata	blue vervain				•
Verbena stricta	hoary vervain			•	
Vernonia fasciculata	ironweed				•
Veronicastrum virginicum	Culver's root				•
Viola pedatifida	prairie violet		•		
Zizia aurea	golden alexanders		•		

Note: Very few = fewer than 50; few = 51–200; moderate = 201–500; high = more than 500.

Glossary

Achene: A single-seed fruit with the seed distinct from the fruit wall.

Alternate leaf arrangement: A single leaf at each stem node. See *opposite leaf arrangement*.

Annual: A plant that germinates from seed, flowers, and sets seeds in the same year.

Basal leaves: Leaves arising from the crown of the plant at ground level.

Bean-shaped seed: A seed that is oval with a rounded lobe on each end.

Bract: A small leaf-like structure just below the disk flower in species of Asteraceae.

Bulb: An underground thickened structure with scales, as in an onion.

Bulblet: A small bulb that forms aboveground.

Calyx: The collective group of leaf-like sepals at the base of a flower.

Capsule: A multisection dry fruit that splits from the top.

Cleistogamous: Referring to flowers that self-fertilize without opening.

Compound leaf: Leaf that is distinctly separated into two or more leaflets.

Compound umbel: An inflorescence consisting of multiple flowers on each flower stalk arising from a common point.

Corm: A bulb-like underground stem with thin papery leaves.

Corymb: A flat or round-topped inflorescence, alternate-branched with lower pedicels longer than the upper.

Crenate: Having V-shaped grooves on the leaf margin; having rounded teeth.

Crown: The base of an herbaceous plant at or just below the ground.

Cylindrical spike head: Having flowers arranged around a cylinder-shaped head as found in the prairie clovers.

Deeply lobed leaf: A simple leaf deeply divided into many segments.

Dentate margin: A leaf edge with teeth pointed outward rather than toward the leaf tip.

Differential seed ripening: Ripe and unripe seeds occurring among and between plants of the same species.

Disk flower: A flower within the circular center of the head on species in the daisy family.

Dissected leaf: A simple leaf deeply divided into many segments.

Double-serrate margin: A leaf margin with two distinctive saw-toothed patterns.

Dry soil: Excessively drained soil.

Dry-mesic soil: Somewhat excessively drained soil.

Elliptic leaf: An oval leaf, broadest in the middle and narrower at two equal ends; width does not exceed half of length.

Entire leaf margin: Continuous leaf edge; not toothed, not notched or divided.

Even-pinnately compound leaf: Compound leaf containing an even number of leaflets.

Few seeds: Production of 51–200 seeds per seed stalk.

Floret: An individual flower within a flower cluster head as in species in the daisy family.

Floss: The white silky threads connected to seeds as found in the milkweed family.

Flower spur: An elongated hollow curved growth as found on the flower of prairie larkspur.

Foliage: Leaves of a plant.

Follicle: A dried fruit containing seeds in a single chamber that splits on one side in milkweed species.

Fused opposing leaves: Opposing leaves physically connected at their base.

Herbaceous plant: Plant whose stems die back at the end of the growing season; not woody.

High seed production: Production of more than 500 seeds per seed stalk.

Husk: A tough outer covering on some fruits and seeds.

Incised vein: Recessed vein on a leaf surface.

Inflorescence: The collective flower cluster on a plant.

Lanceolate/lance-shaped leaf: Leaf shaped like a spear, wide at the base of the leaf blade and tapering to a pointed tip.

Latex sap: A milky sap commonly found in milkweeds.

Leaf axil: The area where the leaf or petiole attaches to the stem.

Leaf blade: The flattened portion of the leaf.

Leaf margin: The outer edge of a leaf.

Leaf scar: The spot on the stem where an attached leaf has fallen off.

Leaf veins: Vascular tissue visible on a leaf surface that is organized in many different patterns.

Leaflet: Leaf-like division of a compound leaf.

Linear-shaped leaf: Long narrow leaf with somewhat parallel sides.

Lodge: To bend over; referring to a seed stalk that is bent over and tangled in adjacent vegetation.

Loment: A segmented pod as in some legumes.

Long duration: Seeds remain on the stalk four weeks or more.

Medium duration: Seeds remain on the stalk up to four weeks.

Mesic soils: Well and moderately well-drained soils.

Midvein: The central vein on the leaf blade.

Moderate seed production: Production of 201–500 seeds per seed stalk.

Notched leaf margin: V-shaped groove along the leaf margins.

Oblanceolate leaf shape: Opposite of lanceolate, with the narrow end of the leaf blade attaching to the petiole or stem.

Odd-pinnately compound leaf: Compound leaf containing an odd number of leaflets.

Opposite leaf arrangement: Two opposing leaves at each stem node. See also *alternate leaf arrangement*.

Oval leaf: A wide elliptic-shaped leaf whose width exceeds one-half its length.

Ovate leaf: Egg-shaped leaf with the wider end connecting to the petiole or stem.

Panicle: A branched inflorescence.

Pappus bristles: A tuft of hair connected to the end of a seed.

Parallel veins: Veins on the leaf surface parallel to the leaf midvein or to each other.

Pea-shaped flower: Flower with a single large upper petal, two side petals, and two lower fused petals common in the bean family.

Pedicel: The stalk of a single flower.

Peduncle: A stalk of a solitary flower.

Petal: A colored segment of the corolla.

Petiole: The leaf stalk.

Pinnate leaflets: Leaflets on both sides of the leaf stalk.

Pod: A dried fruit containing seeds in a single chamber that typically splits into two halves, often found in the bean family.

Puckered leaf venation: Recessed veins on the leaf surface.

Raceme: Unbranched inflorescence with flowers connected by short stems to the main stalk of the plant.

Ray: Strap-like petals surrounding the disk flower of species in the Asteraceae family.

Recurved: Curved backward upon itself.

Reflexed: Bent backward or downward.

Rhizome: A horizontal underground stem that develops into new plants.

Rosette: A dense cluster of radiating leaves at ground level.

Rounded teeth: Referring to serrates on the leaf margin as having rounded rather than pointed tips.

Sepal: Usually a green leaf-like structure at the base of a flower (not in the Asteraceae family).

Serrated teeth: Saw-like teeth along the edge (margin) of a leaf.

Sessile leaf: Leaf attached directly to the main stalk without a petiole.

Short duration: Seeds remain on the stalk for two weeks or less.

Solitary: A single flower or single ray-and-disk flower head on a stalk.

Spike: Unbranched inflorescence with flowers connected directly on the main stalk.

Stalk: The main support structure of the plant.

Stamen: The male organ of the flower.

Stems: Lateral branches of the plant, excluding the main stalk.

Stipule: Paired leaf-like or thread-like appendages at the base of the petiole on plants in the legume family.

Style: The narrow portion of the pistil.

Tepal: A leaf-like structure found on flowers in the lily family; smaller than but not a sepal or a petal.

Twice-divided compound leaf: A compound leaf divided pinnately.

Umbel: The inflorescence consisting of pedicels arising from a common point.

Venation: The pattern of veins on a leaf blade.

Very few seeds: Fewer than fifty seeds produced per seed stalk.

Very short duration: Seeds remain on the stalk for a few days or less.

Wet-mesic soils: Somewhat poorly and poorly drained soils.

Whorl: Three or more leaves arising from a single node.

Winged stalks: Thin and short appendages running the length of the main stalk.

References

Anderson, D. M. 1964. A review of the specific names in North American *Miarus* (Coleoptera: Curculionidae). *Coleopterists' Bulletin* 18:21–24.

Boe, A., B. McDaniel, and K. Robbins. 1989. Direct effect of parasitism by *Dinarmus acutus* Thomson on seed predation by *Acanthoscelides perforatus* (Horn) in Canada milk-vetch. *Journal of Range Management* 42 (6): 514–515.

Boyle, T. H., and K. R. Hladun. 2005. Influence of seed size, testa color, scarification method, and immersion in cool or hot water on germination of *Baptisia australis* (L.) R. Br. seeds. *HortScience* 40:1846–1849.

Britton, N., and A. Brown. 1970. *An illustrated flora of the northern United States and Canada*. New York: Dover Publications.

Christiansen, P., and M. Müller. 1999. *An illustrated guide to Iowa prairie plants*. Iowa City: University of Iowa Press.

Eilers, L. J., and D. M. Roosa. 1994. *The vascular plants of Iowa: An annotated checklist and natural history*. Iowa City: University of Iowa Press.

Haddock, M. 1997–2015. Kansas wildflowers and grasses. Accessed December 10, 2014. http://www.kswildflower.org/.

Harris, J., and M. Harris. 2004. *Plant identification terminology: An illustrated glossary*. Payson, UT: Spring Lake Publishing.

Hilty, J. 2002–2012. Prairie wildflowers of Illinois. Accessed December 10, 2014. http://www.illinoiswildflowers.info/prairie/plant_index.htm.

Kuttruff, J. T., S. G. DeHart, and M. J. O'Brien. 1998. 7500 years of prehistoric footwear from Arnold Research Cave, Missouri. *Science* 281 (5373): 72–75.

Ladd, D., and F. Oberle. 1995. *Tallgrass prairie wildflowers*. Helena, MT: Falcon Press.

Mundahl, N., and K. Plucinski. 2010. Impacts of wild indigo weevil on seed production in longbract wild indigo. *Proceedings of the North American Prairie Conference* 21:163–170.

Pleasants, J., and K. Oberhauser. 2012. Milkweed loss in agricultural fields because of herbicide use: Effect on the monarch butterfly population. *Insect Conservation and Diversity* 6 (2): 135–144.

United States Department of Agriculture, Natural Resources Conservation Service. 2015. PLANTS Database. Accessed December 10, 2014. http://plants.usda.gov.

Williams, D., and B. Butler. 2010. *The Tallgrass Prairie Center guide to seed and seedling identification in the upper Midwest*. Iowa City: University of Iowa Press.

Zhou, X., M. J. Helmers, H. Asbjornsen, R. Kolka, M. D. Tomer, and R. M. Cruse. 2014. Nutrient removal by prairie filter strips in agricultural landscapes. *Journal of Soil and Water Conservation* 69:54–64.

Index